SLAM
the
DOOR
SOFTLY

MARTHA SNYDER BROWN

SLAM *the* DOOR SOFTLY

TATE PUBLISHING
AND ENTERPRISES, LLC

Slam the Door Softly
Copyright © 2015 by Martha Snyder Brown. All rights reserved.

No part of this publication may be reproduced, stored in a retrieval system or transmitted in any way by any means, electronic, mechanical, photocopy, recording or otherwise without the prior permission of the author except as provided by USA copyright law.

The opinions expressed by the author are not necessarily those of Tate Publishing, LLC.

This book is designed to provide accurate and authoritative information with regard to the subject matter covered. This information is given with the understanding that neither the author nor Tate Publishing, LLC is engaged in rendering legal, professional advice. Since the details of your situation are fact dependent, you should additionally seek the services of a competent professional.

Published by Tate Publishing & Enterprises, LLC
127 E. Trade Center Terrace | Mustang, Oklahoma 73064 USA
1.888.361.9473 | www.tatepublishing.com

Tate Publishing is committed to excellence in the publishing industry. The company reflects the philosophy established by the founders, based on Psalm 68:11,
"The Lord gave the word and great was the company of those who published it."

Book design copyright © 2015 by Tate Publishing, LLC. All rights reserved.
Cover design by Joana Quilantang
Interior design by Joana Quilantang

Published in the United States of America
ISBN: 978-1-63449-124-2
Biography & Autobiography / Personal Memoirs
14.12.23

Lovingly dedicated to all the members of
our extended Snyder Family and to "Muzzie"

Foreword

For several years before her death, my mother wrote down incidents from her childhood, intending someday to write a book about the happy times she remembered. After her death, I took the box of notes and held it until I could put them together as she would have wished. When I first looked it over I saw several variations of the same incidents and, not wishing to type and retype, did nothing with it for a long while. With our purchase of a home computer, I realized that I finally had the perfect vehicle with which to recreate my mother's story.

I have included all of the incidents of which she wrote, sometimes compiling the full one from different notes about it. There was much more that she had intended to include but had not yet written. There are pieces of paper with headings such as the following: Circus, Summer Camp, The Bull's Eye, The Bulldog, Swimming, Ice Skating, Dad and the Camera, Visitors Day at Boy Scout Camp, The Operation on the Library Table, Dad Made Furniture, Frisky, Turning Vinegar, High School and George, Stairway Dramatics.

Unfortunately no details were written. I think that it is amazing that she was able to write, in long hand, as much as she did, and it shows how deeply the memories were placed in her heart.

I present it to the family with her love and mine. There is no one whom she would have wished to share it more than her brothers and sisters, and their children and descendants. Her family was the most important thing in her life, as it was in her mother's. She loved them without reservation and completely. She and I are proud to present it to those who never knew the boisterous, energetic, and loving family in which she grew up.

Sincere thanks to my aunt Bea, Beatrice Eleanor Snyder Zimmerman, for patiently trying to recall details ("What house were you in when this happened?"), for looking over the manuscript, and for being so *very* pleased about it.

—Barbara Brown McCusker

"Georgie, Winnie, Noonie, Tommy, Jimmie, Jonnie, Marney, Andy, Bobby, Beacie, Mary, Mother, Daddy." The chant was repeated again and again as each of us tried to outdo the others in speedily naming the members of our family.

It was a hot night in July, and six or seven of our own family were sitting on the front porch trying to catch a breeze. Three were on the porch swing that was held by four chains fastened to strong hooks in the ceiling, Some were lounging on the porch chairs, and friends and neighbor kids who had congregated there were perched on the banisters or the porch steps. Stars twinkled brightly and seemed so close that we wanted to reach out and pull them in to us. The street was quiet except for the creak of a rocking chair here or there on front porches further down. No cars were moving on our street, even though it had only recently been paved.

"Okay, *can* it," ordered Bob, and his rare appearance on the front porch with us younger ones was such a treat that we "canned it" pronto.

The evening was nearing its end now, for most of us still had the summer bedtime curfew of nine o'clock, so the laughter and shouting grew still as someone started singing softly, then another and yet another group joined in.

> Row, row, row your boat
> Gently down the stream.
> Merrily, merrily, merrily, merrily,
> Life is but a dream.

One song followed another and almost always we made a "round" of each song. Even "Twinkle, Twinkle, Little Star" was beautiful when enough of us sang it as a round softly.

Singing was not the *whole* of our lives, but it certainly made up a big part of it.

We had been quite happy in our small house in Penbrook. There were, even then, seven children and Muzzie and Dad. The house—half a double with no central heating and no bathroom—held many memories. Our Muzzie with her delightfully infectious laugh, while Dad was so serious and stern but with a quick mind and a dry sense of humor that tested our own agile brains.

This was the house of pull-taffy parties on crisp fall evenings; of Halloween parties and bobbing for apples in the big washtub; of leaping from warm snuggly beds onto the icy floor, grabbing our clothes and racing downstairs to dress beside the big black kitchen stove; of sitting around the big kitchen table on various sizes and shapes of chairs and stools to do our homework, the "older" ones helping the "younger" ones; of the excitement and anticipation watching Dad build our huge bobsled and that perfect test run with Dad riding in front, yelling "Whee-ee-ee-ee! It's a beaut!"

This was the house of hikes and picnics in the summer and riding the trolley car to the park; of Thanksgiving and two chickens roasted brown and beautiful in the great black stove—and that rare Thanksgiving when we could afford a *turkey*; and of Christmas—the exchange of hand-made gifts, the luscious candies and cookies Muzzie had made and hidden (she thought) from us so that there would be plenty on "the Day," the one gift from Santa and an *orange* so rare and precious, and Christmas carols sounding off from all parts of the house. This was the house from which we took long hikes into the country, in all seasons, with Dad (Muzzie too if she was not too close to term with a new baby) and *always* had the nightly reading from the Bible by Dad, followed by all of us kneeling beside Muzzie and Dad to say our prayers.

In this house, Saturday nights never varied. Great kettles of water were heated on the cookstove and poured into the big washtub standing on the floor, the cold water added from the pump to bring it to the right temperature. All was ready. It was bath night.

Three of us little ones could fit into the tub, rather a tight squeeze, but Muzzie would kneel beside the tub and scrub us for dear life while Dad stood ready with the towel. He who was out of the tub first was lucky—the towel was nice and dry. The older ones had to wait for more water to heat so that they could bathe alone. They were modest. Finally bath night was over, and the next day was Sunday.

On this the Sabbath Day, after a quick but filling breakfast of mush and milk or fried mush with molasses, which was a favorite, it was time to finish dressing.

Then the "inspection" came. Muzzie and Dad were sticklers for cleanliness. "Cleanliness is next to Godliness,'" they insisted, and there was no getting around it. Inspection by them was stiff. We stood in line just inside the front door. No one left the house with even the tiniest smudge or stain for they would spot it and the culprit would cringe under the hard gazes of our inspectors.

But at last we were ready, and two by two, a little one holding onto the hand of a bigger one, we paraded to Sunday school and church.

Before their marriage, Mother was a firm Baptist and Dad a slightly Reformed, so in fairness and justice to all (?) they became a merged Lutheran.

Dad was a pillar of the church, and we were proud of him. He was a member of the board and superintendent of the adult Sunday school. Needless to say we were extra well behaved because everything we did was reported to him. But all in all, we were a reverent bunch. We learned our books of the Bible and our Sunday school lessons easily, no doubt because one of our punishments for misdemeanors at home was, frequently, to learn by heart a Bible verse— and be able to recite it at any moment.

After Sunday school, we all made a beeline for the lavatories, located in little houses behind the church, then back again to sit primly in a row beside Dad, for this was Muzzie's moment.

She sang in the choir, at least when she was not too far advanced with child. At those times, she sat in our pew and yearned to be in the choir loft. She had a beautiful voice, and we were proud of her, but it was nice to sit beside her too for then we felt like a complete family. She was, ordinarily, a tiny person, but her voice was big and beautiful— as big and beautiful as her faith in God, and she sang His praises with a love and joy that knew no bounds.

Every night, we had wonderful Bible-reading sessions! Few people whom I've ever heard read the Bible, including ministers, had the wondrous ability to bring all those people alive as my father had. He had Jonah and the whale and the wild stormy ocean right there beside us in the sitting room. We sat spellbound, quiet as mice, fearful that Dad might give us only a part of the story that night and continue it the next.

One night, as the story was in progress, I caught Andy holding his nose with one hand and raising the other hand above his head as he slid quietly from the chair to the floor. He was pretending to be like Jonah, and I spoiled it all with a giggle. I couldn't help it. But that ended the story for that night.

The book clicked shut. Dad bowed his head, and we quickly followed suit. He and Muzzie said their prayer, and we all said "Amen." Then in unison we children prayed, kissed them goodnight and reluctantly scooted upstairs to our cold beds. But two small bodies wriggling about from side to side soon warmed the coldest bed, and in no time we were asleep.

Our ancestry was German-English-Dutch, which by the time it reached us was ground up and watered down so much that we were just plain Americans. Actually we were, if anything, just plain Pennsylvania Dutch, although none of us could speak it. Muzzie and Dad were able to say all sorts of things in front of us in complete safety from our prying ears.

We tanned so deeply in the summer that our friends were never quite sure of our ancestry. Our dark-brown, almost black, hair, dark complexions, and tall, lean frames made our fictional Midwestern Indian ancestors seem more likely, as we circulated the rumor often enough and basked in its "myth" most of our growing-up years. Knowing one of us, you recognized the rest of us anywhere. We had so close a resemblance that outsiders seldom were able to call us by our right names without some stuttering hesitation. Our own Muzzie often ran through half our names before settling on the name she wanted to call.

Dad was a federal bank examiner, and we were proud of him. The oldest of five children, he had only attended the first eight grades of public school before he was forced to drop out. After that, he'd gone to work and attended night school when he could. Still later, he worked in a bank, starting at the bottom and slowly, tenaciously worked his way up. Then he took a civil service exam and became an assistant bank examiner. After he and Muzzie married, he continued to read and study, and though many of us eventually graduated from college, he remained by far the smartest of us all.

Muzzie had also attended eight grades of public school when, as the oldest of nine children, she went to work because her family needed her help. She was tiny, with raven black hair and big soft brown eyes. She was so slim when they were married that Dad could encircle his two hands around her waist and was a real beauty with a love for every living creature. She had a beautiful soprano voice and sang in her church choir at Harrisburg. Here her voice was so greatly appreciated that a group of businessmen approached her with an offer to finance her in three or four years of study abroad. It was tremendously tempting, but she'd fallen in love and she and Dad were married.

Theirs was a good, long love—the kind that gives confidence to the children born within its encircling arms. They loved each other, and us, dearly.

Their first home was a little house consisting of two rooms, one up and one down. But they soon had to move into larger quarters, on Penn Street in Penbrook, for the babies began to arrive. A family of eleven children, even in my day, was considered a big one, and for being a Lutheran family, ours was really big. We were not really a *goal* of Muzzie and Dad, such as "We'll have half a dozen children" or "We'll settle for a full dozen." But when the stork found our house, he just continued to call back every two years, and we just grew and grew and grew.

Mary was the first, a roly-poly charmer who laughed a lot and probably always had the best disposition of the bunch.

SLAM THE DOOR SOFTLY

Next was Ruthie, our two-week-old sister whom we never knew. A neighbor was helping Muzzie with the baby and giving her a bath near the back door. The neighbor's small son kept running in and out of the door, and because it was during the winter, Ruthie caught pneumonia and died. Muzzie never blamed her neighbor but always mourned not being able to raise her daughter.

After that, in succession, came Beatrice, Robert, and Andrew, and the house *definitely* became too small. Dad and Muzzie found a slightly larger house at 234 South 29th Street in Penbrook, to which Martha, John, and James arrived each in their turn.

When I was born, a neighbor asked Bob if he'd trade his new baby sister for a parrot. "Oh yes!" he said eagerly. "It can talk, and all she does is cry." He couldn't really be blamed. Babies were a common commodity at our house, and being the fifth was not exactly a highlight but rather a problem—where shall we stow this one?

The question was always solved by each child moving over one more bed and one more chair. This was better than it sounds, for no one child was stuck for more than two years with the old gray backless chair.

My oldest sister, Mary, became conscious of the incongruity of this piece of furniture when she was twelve and had invited a new friend to our house for dinner. She must have suffered mightily during the meal for, after her friend had departed, she burst into tears. "Oooohhh, Mother!" she cried. "Why must we have that *blasted* thing here in the kitchen? I was *never* so *mortified*!" Her voice rose dramatically as she took full note of her ready-made audience, and her tears flowed as she compared our hodgepodge kitchen/dining room furniture with her friend's matched dining-room suite.

What she said? "*Blasted!*" That was as good as any swear word to us little ones. We stared wide eyed, sucking in our breaths with horrified delight and, at the same time, hopefully perking up our ears for more.

"Mary!" Muzzie scolded. "First of all, that is *not* good language. Secondly, and you'd better learn this now, people come to our house because they like *us*, not our furniture. And third, how would your father cut the boys' hair if we didn't have that backless chair?"

That seemed fair enough to us. How could Dad put the small stool, reserved for raising the little ones to his "cutting" level, on a chair with a back? He couldn't. Not another chair in the house had such a broad bottom nor held us all prisoners of our father-barber so securely.

Mary sniffed unhappily. She had no answer, for there wasn't any, but she was far from satisfied. "Well, you can be sure I'll have no backless chairs in my home," she sniffed and stalked majestically from the room.

She wouldn't be gone for long. The rest of the house was late-November cold, and despite the low fire kept burning in the pot-bellied sitting room stove, that room was almost as cold as the unheated rest of the house.

Only the kitchen was warm and cozy. The big black cookstove of seemingly gigantic proportions radiated warmth like great flexible arms of love, and we navigated toward it as blissfully as baby chicks to their mother. It was pure glutton for wood and coal, but as it took, so it gave. Atop the hot surface was always to be seen anywhere from one to five kettles, pots, or pans, with a possible pot roast in one, placed on the back of the stove for long slow cooking. The huge black frying pan held fresh fried potatoes and sliced onions crackling and sizzling to a crispy brown, which filled the air with such drooling delight that we could

SLAM THE DOOR SOFTLY

scarcely wait to pick up our forks. And oh, that homemade vegetable soup! And on or around it could also be found at various times bread, cakes, pies, drying mittens, underwear, and diapers.

Balanced diet? We never heard of it. In those days of no central heating, you dressed for cold weather and ate food that "put meat on your bones." Besides that, we had no bathroom. You had to be husky and well-padded to make that mad dash in near-zero weather from the kitchen door out to that little house. So we ate well—snitz & knepp, sauerkraut and mashed potatoes, fritters, dumplings, doughnuts, pies, cakes, and cookies. But none of us ever walked anywhere—we *ran*, so there was no chance to be overweight.

Kerosene lamps were used exclusively because our house was not piped for gas, and of course, there was no such thing as electricity. We had special jobs to perform in the care of the lamps, the older children washing the chimneys and keeping the wicks trimmed, while the younger ones made the trip to the store for the coal oil. My first real memory was when as a little girl of four years I took the kerosene can to the grocery store and asked for "coy yoil." For this mispronunciation the grocer, Mr. Small, never failed to laugh heartily and reach into one of his big candy jars for a long strip of my favorite—licorice with pink, yellow, and white dots of luscious hard candy. What a reward!

At the end of two weeks of summer Bible school at our church, all who had attended regularly had the dubious honor of performing for their doting parents, relatives, and friends—all of whom were what is known as a captive audience. None of them really *wanted* to sit through the thing any more than *we* wanted to perform for them.

One unforgettable skit was entitled *Mother Suds Family*, about a washer woman and her large brood of children gathered around a big wooden washtub filled with *soap suds*.

What a mess! All of us were soaking wet by the time the skit was over!

We put on home plays, all of us taking turns as actors while the others were the audience. Dad and Muzzie took their turns as often as we did and had a bang-up time whichever side of the screen they chose.

These two caused a near riot one evening when they were the actors. Dad hung an old sheet in the archway between the two small living rooms—our divider between stage and auditorium—then he turned up the wicks in three coal oil (kerosene) lamps and placed them on the table behind the "actors," and we sat on rows of chairs in the dark "auditorium."

They had promised us a "very interesting" performance, and we sat tall and big eyed, watching the "screen." But nothing happened. There was no sound, either from behind the screen or from the audience. Tension mounted. We watched—and waited—and the "little ones" began to wiggle and squirm as we "hushed" them. Still nothing happened.

Then the silhouette of a man appeared on the right of the screen, walking very slowly toward the center. A second later, the silhouette of a woman appeared on the left, walking to meet the man. The man was holding something in his hands—a piece of wood? No, he was lifting a lid on top of the "thing." A box? Yes! A box! The man held out the box to the lady, and she, very slowly and dramatically, picked something from the box, lifted it slowly, and delicately to her lips and began to chew, clasping her hands together in sheer delight. Then the man took something from the box and—but bedlam had broken out in the audience!

"Candy! Candy!" we shrieked, and, a big one swooping up a little one, rushed onstage, nearly knocking the actors down in our attempt to reach the candy, and Muzzie and Dad clinging to each other weak with laughter.

That was the shortest play we ever had—but oh, that chocolate-covered candy!

In Penbrook, we first had an organ that Muzzie knew how to play a little bit and on which she taught Mary to play some hymns. Later, Dad traded it for a piano, and Mary, nine years old, and Bea, six years old, started piano lessons from Mr. Baker, who lived across the street. Bea soon rebelled and played by ear thereafter.

Bob and Andy, seven and five at the time, were given two rabbits by a farmer we knew and hurried home to show the family. "One for each of us," cried Andy, holding his scared brown bunny against his chest.

"Look, Muzzie," Bob said pleadingly. He was not nearly so naive as Andy and knew the rule at our house.

"Pets are nice," Dad had said every time we wanted one, "but there is no room for them."

"See," Bob went on, "only two rabbits. We could build them a pen out in the yard and you'll never know they're there. Please…"

Mother and Dad looked at one another. "Only two," said Dad, with a wry grin.

Muzzie sighed. "But for how long?" They conferred silently just looking at one another. Then Dad nodded and Mother shrugged.

"You have full responsibility for feeding and watering them," Dad said sternly.

The boys nodded eagerly. "Oh yes, we will."

"And clean out the hutch—twice a week."

"Yes, yes."

Dad built the hutch, a really nice one, and the two boys cared for their pets, and the two bunnies were happy. They grew and grew, and the hutch was built bigger and bigger because they multiplied and multiplied. The final total, as close as we could count, was fifty one.

Dad and Muzzie began to worry, but just in the nick of time, the problem was solved. Dad was transferred to another town. This meant that we would have to move—and we couldn't take the rabbits along.

"No, definitely not," Dad said flatly.

We all stood close in a united group, as was our custom during our times of stress, and Bob, a worried eight-year-old at the time, asked "But what'll we do with them?"

Dad spoke without thinking, his mind already on bigger things, like the right moving company to contact or finding a house in the new location, and as soon as he spoke, he was sorry. "Oh, we'll have rabbit stew, I guess…" Then he saw our faces—shocked, incredulous, and indignant, our united loyalties fleeing quickly from him to the big family even now nestled snug in their hutch in the backyard.

That was probably the only time I ever saw Dad embarrassed. He tried to reassure us that he'd only been "joshing," but we couldn't be sure. "I'll take them out to Mr. Kreitzer's farm, and they'll have a happy time of it out there," he said then shook his head firmly. "Don't look at me like that. That's the very best I can do, and that's *that*."

Needless to say, we watched the hutch closely thereafter, checking carefully to see that all fifty-one members of the family were accounted for. And even then, we couldn't be sure that one or two, or even three, weren't missing. They hopped around so much it was almost impossible to make an accurate count.

Each meal after that, we watched suspiciously as the meat platter was put on the table. As long as we were reasonably sure that the meat was ham or beef or fish, we ate. But if it bore even a faint resemblance to rabbit, as chicken did, we panicked and suddenly lost our appetites. We *knew* that Muzzie wouldn't do that to us, but we couldn't be sure.

Only when Mr. Kreitzer actually carried off the rabbits—hutch and all—in his big wagon did our appetites really return, and then we are like starved refugees.

Ten year-old Bea had just received her first lesson in the art of crochet, and wanting to be alone in peace and quiet, she went out to sit on the roof of the rabbit hutch. Probably the real reason she went out there was to keep out of sight in case Muzzie wanted her to do some work. Also, probably the bathroom was occupied. She worked with painstaking concentration for a full fifteen minutes and then, sitting cross-legged on the hutch, began doodling with the hook. Somehow she embedded it in the ball of her bare foot.

She didn't scream or cry. An Indian doesn't show pain, and we always had to be stoical like Indians, but in a normal voice, she called Bob to come out and showed him the hook buried in her foot. "Bob will be a doctor one day," Muzzie always said, and in truth, it was he who always took care of the hurts and helped the doctor. He settled down beside her, and slowly, gently, and carefully, he turned and twisted and finally removed the deeply embedded steel crochet hook

Dogs were forbidden, but somehow we seemed to attract them, and moments were rare when we were without one kind of a mongrel or another. A pedigree dog was out of the question—Dad and Muzzie would never have *paid* for a dog—and they were delicate. Muzzie had enough "caring for the sick" with colicky babies, earaches, colds, measles, mumps, chicken pox, etc., etc., in her own brood without the added responsibility of a pedigreed animal to pull through one illness or another.

But Tony, a Heinz 57 variety, was the one dog for which Muzzie ever felt a real love. Dad had always been against having any pets because there were so many of us, but Bob wanted Tony so badly that he consulted with Muzzie, who finally advised him to write a letter to Dad. He did and said, "He is a nice dog. He is a *he* dog." Bob got his dog. His ancestry was vague and as spotty as his coat. We loved him dearly.

The front porch on our house had no banister. One day, Muzzie had put Jimmie on the porch in the carriage for a nap, and Tony was lying in the shade under it. A sudden windstorm came up. Muzzie sent one of us for the little ones, another for the baby, and others to close the windows, while she and several older ones raced to the backyard to take the clothes off the line. A strong gust began to roll the baby carriage off the porch. Tony grabbed its handle with his teeth and hung on for dear life until someone rushed outside and rescued them both. We all made much of Tony that day. He was a real hero!

When Andy was six years old and Bob was eight, Andy caught his hand in a corn husker. Bob had to put a hand

and a foot on the big cogwheel to hold it and reach with his other hand to turn it off. Another time the two of them were sliding down a steep shale bank. Bob pushed Andy, and Andy fell on his face all the way to the bottom, tearing a piece out of the bridge of his nose. He went back the next week to find it and did.

Once, Tom was riding down Highland Avenue on his sleigh. It stopped, but Tom kept on going and ended up with cinders ground into his face.

Even Jim fell from a billboard and broke his arm.

It was no wonder that Muzzie frequently sighed, "Give me strength!"

During the First World War, the flu epidemic slashed through our town like a knife. She had seven children then and was aware of the danger to them, but her neighbors were *dying*. She trusted in God—boiled our water and scrubbed herself before entering and upon leaving the sick. She saved *eight* families. Then when they were recovering, it struck her. She recovered but grieved about her lost unborn baby.

Just before Tommy arrived, Dad was promoted and transferred to Sunbury, Pennsylvania. Dad had made several trips to Sunbury to find and rent us a house, but each time he mentioned the size of his family, the potential landlord just shook his head and turned away. After looking at six houses and speaking with six landlords, when the sixth one refused, he was really desperate. He knew he'd have to use new tactics for the next one because it was his last chance. There were no more houses for rent in Sunbury.

The landlord, a Mr. Hoffman, was a bachelor and quite old and sour, we discovered much later. He showed Dad the house that he considered to be a palace and was actually one-half a double and asked his questions in a whining wheedling tone of voice. Dad gave his answers, but he had his own thoughts about the questions.

"You're married?"

"Oh yes," Dad replied cheerfully. *The old dummy. What would a single man want with a whole house?*

"Your wife clean?"

"Oh, indeed!" Dad affirmed, inwardly doing a slow burn but still smiling. "She's immaculate."

"You have a steady job?"

"Yes. I work for the government—civil service." *That'll make him sit up and take notice, the old buzzard.*

Apparently it did bring a weak smirk of pleasure to the landlord's face. But the next question was the bomb, and Dad was waiting for it.

"Have any children?"

Dad looked him straight in the eye and said, "Yes. We have a daughter fifteen years old and a son two years old."

This was satisfactory. Two children of such ages would not do any damage to his precious house, and certainly they would not be noisy and disturb his tenants on the other side. The rent was paid, and the keys exchanged hands. Dad had rented us a house!

The move to Sunbury, population fifteen thousand in November of 1920, was a momentous and fearful adventure for all of us children, but even as we chewed our nails in worry for what the future held for us, we reveled in the long train ride of fifty-four miles. We looked out the windows on both sides of the car at once, marveling at all the new and interesting sights, and at the same time sat as close to Muzzie and Dad as we could get, hoping that a few of the knots in our stomach would dissolve.

Each click of the wheels on the rails seemed to speak, saying the same phrases we'd said to each other.

"We're going to the city."

"Scary."

"Will we like it?"

"Will we look like country hicks?"

"Will we have friends?"

"Is everybody here?"

I suspect that the older ones were a little hopeful too, feeling that one or two could well get lost so they'd not look like freaks on arrival in our "new life" that Mary mentioned so often.

Moving day arrived, and so did we! Despite all of Muzzie's hushing as we explored the house, we probably sounded like a herd of elephants to our neighbors on the other side of the wall. And no doubt the flushing toilet sounded to them like a broken water main, but the little ones just couldn't resist testing this marvelous invention in the marvelous *bathroom* each time they passed. After all, new things were to be tested and, if possible, taken apart for thorough exploration.

We lugged and carried and rushed upstairs and down, putting things in order, while Muzzie directed traffic. By nightfall, we were settled in. The meal was cold but ready, all beds were made, and the family Bible was in place on the library table. Then at last the "little ones" were "prayered" and tucked into bed, the last dish put into the cupboard, and the remainder of our exhausted family fell into their beds.

The next day was the beginning of one great treasure hunt for the little ones, and each new discovery brought them to the kitchen door to shout their news to the older ones, who were working inside at the tremendous job of "putting on the finishing touches."

"There's a big grape arbor in the back, Mamie," Jonnie piped. "I bet I can climb up and walk on the top."

Mary nearly fell off the step ladder in the dining room where she'd been hanging curtains. "No," she cried. "Don't you dare try that! Now mind! You stay earthbound today, or" she threatened, "you'll get a hot bottom."

Bea, upstairs with Muzzie, was hanging bedroom curtains and doing a lot of grunting and groaning. She hated housework and wanted desperately to get outside on her own to investigate the new neighborhood.

Muzzie had listened to her fussing long enough. "All right, Beatrice," she said firmly. "You are holding yourself back. Do your job *right*, and you can go outside. Otherwise you'll be here all day."

Bea sighed heavily but knew that the law was the law. However, she couldn't resist the chance to whisper a forbidden "Drat it," when the curtain rod slipped and fell to the floor.

But the noisiest spot was in the kitchen. Dad was *trying* to put the big black cookstove together so we could eat again, *and* have some hot water. Bob and Andy were assisting, but now and then, some of the parts would fall to the floor with a great crash because, well, Dad wasn't really a mechanic. Then the air grew electric, waiting for his temper to fly.

Amazingly, he held his peace but still gave orders to Bob and Andy in the tone of a drill sergeant. "Hold it there, Bobby. That's right. No—don't drop it. Andy, get that big bolt and the nut that goes with it. No—over there."

Dad was holding one heavy section of the stove and had no hands to point, so he lifted his right foot and aimed it toward the nut and bolt lying on the floor.

There were no screens in any of the windows or doors at that point, and all kinds of insects had felt welcome in our midst. Just at that point—Dad standing on one foot, holding the "iron devil" as he called it, and pointing the other foot—a misguided hornet zoomed onto his foot and buried his fangs.

The clash and clatter of the falling iron devil was nothing compared to the scream of agony and the long unmentionable sentence that came from Dad as he hopped around on one foot, holding the other in a sheer grip of death. The only printable word was "Consarn" it. Everyone raced to the scene, and seven pairs of eyes grew huge as we stood in a circle around him.

Mother arrived far in the lead and threw orders thick and fast.

"Bobby, get a chair for your father.

"Daddy, sit down.

"Mary, go to the neighbor—take this bucket—and ask if we may please have some very hot water. Hurry now.

"Beacie, run up to the bathroom closet and get the ichthyol salve.

"Marney, be sure the little ones stay outside—down at the end of the yard would be best." Then glancing at Dad, she added, "You'd better stay with them.

"Bobby and Andy, take the other two buckets and a broom for each—the scrubbing brooms—and scrub the front porch.

"Hurry now!" She bent down to lift and examine Dad's foot.

It probably did hurt badly, but Dad seemed to us to be enjoying this concentrated attention. He was putting on a fine act and prolonging the agony beyond the limit he would allow any of us to moan.

Bob and Andy, on the front porch, were reluctant to begin the scrubbing job. The one open window was an excellent listening post, and both leaned over the sill as far as they could go—with their posteriors and slowly waving legs showing the public a fine picture of the art of balancing.

"He's not saying anything now," Andy whispered.

"Shush," Bob cautioned.

"We're supposed to be scrubbing."

Mary hurried back across the street, carrying a half bucket of water, followed by an obliging neighbor who was carefully carrying a tea kettle from which steam was still rising. Both completely ignored the eavesdroppers as they went around the side of the house to the kitchen.

"Who's that?" Bob hissed.

"Miss Stein—lives across the street," Andy informed him. "She's a schoolteacher."

Bob backed off the window sill and slid down to the porch.

Andy turned, "Watsa matter?"

"No use listening now. Dad won't dare cuss with her there. Hah, a schoolteacher."

Andy nodded. "Across the street too," he added glumly.

Needless to say, Dad did recover, but as we all anticipated, he ran *our* legs off on (to us) unnecessary errands so that he could rest *his* leg. He was aided and abetted by Muzzie, who babied him beyond belief and made sure his bandage was big and fat and *very* noticeable. Two male neighbors from up the street came in and put the stove together so that once again Muzzie could cook and we could eat.

It was from this house that we greeted Sunbury—loud and clear—and Sunbury watched us for awhile, then took us to her bosom.

As time passed, we found that we had "lovely neighbors," as Muzzie said, adding sternly and staring at each one of us as we sat at dinner, "and I want it to *stay* that way."

As a matter of fact, we did have good neighbors up and down the street, but there was one neighbor who found us a little more than she could swallow, possibly because she had us morning noon and night—separated only by a thin wall.

Poor Mrs. Fornwald, she was a very delicate woman, as was her husband. But the most delicate of all was their son.

Every day after the first few weeks (we figured they were allowing us that time as a "settling in" period), Mr. Fornwald came to the front door, asked to see Muzzie, and made the same request word for word. "Please, Mrs. Snyder, will you ask your children to walk, not run, through the upstairs hall. My wife is ill again." He then tipped his hat, turned, and walked off the porch and down the street to his work.

Poor Muzzie was upset to the point that she too became almost ill and, once again tried to impress upon us that we *must* be quiet. "After all, the Fornwalds have equal rights, and you are being very selfish."

Knowing that she now must make a superhuman effort, even as she disliked using the threat, she finally said it: "The next child who runs through the upstairs hall—at any time—will be reported to your father when he gets home this weekend."

That did it. Such a threat from Muzzie was unbelievable for she determined that Dad should have peaceful and happy weekends at home and had, up to now, always coped with our problems without reporting our worst transgressions to Dad. She much preferred that he believe that we were angels all week long.

Thus began a long period of tiptoeing through the upstairs hall—three years of it to be exact—and still Mrs. Fornwald was "poorly" and their son remained "delicate.

Four-year-old Jonnie climbed every tree in the neighborhood. He and Marney swung on the grape arbor so violently that the vine broke and both flew backwards, struck their heads on the pavement, and were knocked out cold. They revived.

Twelve-year-old Beatrice, tomboy to the core, played a harder game of baseball than any boy on the neighborhood boy's team, walked every back fence with perfect balance, and constantly bewailed the fact that she was a girl. But her greatest sin—"undoing all my efforts toward being a good neighbor," so Muzzie said—was to beat up the neighborhood "sissy." She wasn't sorry, but Muzzie led her to their front door, and she had to apologize to his highly indignant mother.

Two-year-old, almost three, Jimmie was lost twice and was found both times through the "flushing out" system the neighborhood kids had devised before we moved in. They circled the block, stationed themselves at intervals, and all worked inward, somewhat like a chicken roundup. Jimmie was both times somewhere within the circle—once sitting in the middle of a very dusty empty lot, playing quietly and alone with his small fire truck, and the second time sitting in a neighbor's kitchen, happily eating cookies and drinking milk.

Ten-year-old Bob began his own business of hauling market baskets with his express wagon for women who had bought more than they had intended at the farmers' market. This paid off quite well.

Eight-year-old Andy of the brittle bones continued with his accidents—a mashed finger, courtesy of Marney, whom he was chasing through the house and who got through the door fast enough to slam it behind her, right on his finger.

Aunt Mable arrived from Texas on her way to her job in Washington, DC, detouring on the train to see her long-unseen sister and her family. Muzzie had the table full of freshly baked pies ready and waiting. Aunt Mable took a piece of each, kissed each one of us between bites, and then hurried to catch her train. The sisters were laughing and crying and kissing. She was our favorite aunt!

Our first Sunday in the new town was normal in all respects. Everybody was up bright and early, breakfast on the double, and full speed ahead on washing and dressing. Luckily, Muzzie insisted on the Saturday-night rule of laying out our clothes for Sunday school. That way, any last-minute repairs could be made, and too, if someone had outgrown his clothes during the week, there was still time to pass them down the line. Of course, this could have unhappy results for the oldest of that sex. He might have passed on his pants or shirt so the fast-growing one down the line could be clothed and end up with nothing to wear.

But that first Sunday morning all went well. Final inspection over, we filed out the door and down the street. We were a rather nice-looking procession, Dad carrying the baby, Muzzie leading the next youngest by the hand,

and the rest of us walking ahead by twos, an older one taking charge of a younger one.

Many a curtain moved restlessly at living room windows as we passed down the street, and we knew that people were saying "There goes that new family down the street. *My*, aren't there a lot of them?"

I was too young to feel anything but pride in us. I loved the fullness of our ranks. But Mary and Bea squirmed uncomfortably all the way downtown, and I could hear them muttering, "Making a bloody spectacle of ourselves. We could at least travel in shifts!"

One person who did *not* take us to his bosom—beside our landlord who was still speechless from Dad's evasion of the "whole truth"—was the minister of the Zion Lutheran Church. "He never came to call." This was an insult which, in an earlier century, would have brought on a challenge for a duel, and Dad would have been the challenger.

Muzzie and Dad were shocked beyond belief and *never, never* set foot inside that church again. Dad was a "never forgiver or forgetter," and Muzzie was his wife and was *loyal*, so she would not go to church if Dad would not. Muzzie was forced to lose the most important part of her life outside of her family, and despite all her efforts to smile over it, her hurt was deep and sad and forever. She lost church but never God!

I'm sure that Dad ached inside because he was keeping her home. I know too that he lost a great piece of his own life in denying himself the joy of attending church, but he was proud and unbending. He never spoke that minister's name, and we never said it in his presence.

But *we* fixed the minister. We children descended on his church in a body to Sunday school and later to church, spilling out all over the place, joining everything, singing forcefully and praying with religious fervor. We became the most active members he ever had.

However, we didn't go en masse as before. Perhaps it was the metropolitan atmosphere in that huge town of fifteen thousand, or maybe it was because we didn't have the parental eye upon us going to and from the church. For whatever reason, we decided that ten cents was too much to put into the collection plate and that five cents would do just as well. The other nickel was pure profit. After Sunday school, we made a beeline to the drugstore on the next corner and invested in some necessary candy.

Many years later, he proved Dad's opinion that "he's no Christian and should not be in that pulpit," to be correct. The minister was more than indiscreet with a lady of the parish and was sent packing. Dad felt quite sanctimonious at this denouncement and subsequent dismissal of the minister, but the die was cast. He never again went to church.

Meanwhile, Dad and Muzzie laid the groundwork toward being longtime residents of Sunbury. They "screened" the local doctors, dentists, butchers, bakers, shoe-repairmen, and merchants and settled on those whom they felt were the best—regardless of price, and those "chosen" ones welcomed us with open arms. No doubt about it, we were a gold mine to any community.

The doctor, *dear* Dr. Thomas, or "Dr. Tommy," as Dad and Muzzie called him, was probably the most overworked man of our choice. It was he who came, day or night, when an earache was beyond Muzzie's control. It was he who lanced our boils, set our broken bones, stitched us together, and wrapped us in miles of bandages.

And when once again we were expecting a baby, it was Dr. Thomas who delivered him and admired him along with the rest of us.

Tommy was our first baby born in Sunbury and the first born in a hospital and was named of course for the good doctor. Since it was a biblical name also, it was the perfect choice.

The next time Muzzie was expecting a baby, she was having some unusual pains, and Dad finally convinced her that Dr. Thomas should come to the house to check her. Afterward, he insisted that Muzzie have her baby at the hospital when the time came.

He told Muzzie and Dad, "It will be much better for everyone. You Carrie will have a complete rest." He grinned. "Probably the first one you ever had, so take advantage of it. And"—he turned to Dad—"it will give you some idea of what she goes through here, with this covey of wild birds." As a final parting shot to Dad, he added, "It won't be easy. But you'll be fine."

Dad met his grin with an annoyed humph, and then as he opened the front door for the doctor, he added his own parting shot. "Little you know about it. We'll be just fine. Drop in some day. You'll see."

Dr. Thomas stopped in the doorway and turned to look Dad straight in the eye. "Is that an invitation or a dare?"

Dad had no intention of letting "Tommy" know that his humor was highly appreciated, so he waved a brusque hand, and the doctor continued out, over the porch and down the steps, shoulders shaking and hand over his mouth.

But Dr. Tommy was concerned, and when he was called to the house the following week, he ordered Muzzie to bed. After seeing that she was settled and lying flat in bed, he came downstairs to us. He looked around at the circle of frightened faces, and then nodded his head.

"Your mother *must* stay in bed for *one week*," he said, "and maybe longer if she can't have peace and quiet." He looked intently at each of us. "You may lose the new baby, and your mother may be terribly ill, or worse, *unless*"—he emphasized each word—"*you help each other down here—and keep quiet.*"

Dad was out of town, but he came immediately at our SOS. A practical nurse was called in, and she took complete charge. It was a whispering, tiptoeing week with each of us casting frightened looks upward at every tiny sound. More prayers were said than ever before!

That one week of total rest was just what Mother needed. Three weeks later, she went to the Mary M. Packer Hospital, and Vernon was born. And he was number nine.

One kid in our block was a sissy and, since he was the same age as Bea, she took it upon herself to beat him up at least once or twice a week. One day, she started out of our backyard to go over to his yard and call him out. She had the habit of jumping over the fence gate instead of opening it, and this particular day, she caught her foot and fell flat on her face.

Our nice next-door neighbor, Mr. Cooke, saw her fall and came running to pick her up. She was too embarrassed to admit that she wasn't hurt and lay quite swooningly in his arms as he quickly carried her into our house.

One of our boys called, "Bea's hurt," and heads raised all along the way as Mr. Cooke carried his limp burden through the kitchen, dining room, and into the living room. Eyes raised from the sandbox, from the dishes in the sink, from the homework on the dining room table, eyes wide with concern. No one spoke.

In the living room, Muzzie was holding a colicky baby on the rocking chair. With one motion, she handed me the baby, indicated that I should rock him, helped put Bee on the couch, and began to feel and probe for broken bones and bumps. Head, neck, arms, legs, gently but firmly, those knowing hands would ferret out any injury. But she found none.

She looked at Bea's face, studied it, and then straightened up again. "Thank you very much, Mr. Cooke. I think she'll be all right. I'll just put an ice pack on her head and keep her in bed for the rest of the day" Ugh! What a punishment! And it was only one o'clock in the afternoon!

Balancing was part of growing up. An upended broom balanced on the forefinger was "fair" to "good," depending on how long the balancer could keep it up (and the porch or pavement that the balancer was originally set outside to sweep got a "lick and a promise.") If Muzzie sent one of us for a yardstick or a ruler, the messenger invariably returned teetering and swaying with his full attention on the stick balanced on his finger.

Lids for the pots and pans were great items to balance on the head, though if Muzzie caught us, we had to wash and dry the lid before putting it away.

When seven-year-old Jonnie was given the job of pushing the current baby in the carriage on the front porch until it was asleep, he never failed to see more enticing things to do with his time. So he would stand at one end of the porch and give the carriage one great shove toward the other end and then leap down the steps and race down the street and out of sight. When the carriage crashed into the opposite banister, the unsuspecting and drowsy baby put up a terrific howling and Muzzie came a-running. But Jonnie was gone, not to return until dinner time!

We lasted three years in that house, to the dismay of our poor landlord, who was constantly wringing his hands over his "destructive tenants." Finally, our landlord stopped wringing his hands and *asked* us to move! Dad was so furious that he went out and, by golly, *bought* a house! We didn't want his old house anyway.

Dad bought a single house at 1236 Race Street. Joy! It wasn't big enough, of course, but it was elastic. One bathroom became a problem, for our family continued to grow. The boys ganged up on the girls and "took over" the bathroom until everyone was allotted a specific time. Not everyone stuck to the schedule, however, especially Andy, who was always in there for at least an hour. It was probably the only place he could get any privacy.

In our family, the VIPs were, of course, Muzzie and Dad, but we the offshoots were very important too—no doubt because we all had good lungs and were quite willing to voice our opinions. Table conversation on those leisurely evenings when no one had to rush off somewhere were very likely to become discussions, and more often than not, they would turn into heated arguments in which everyone took sides. Of course, when Dad rapped on the table, all heated arguments stopped.

"Discuss," Muzzie told us. "Listen to the other side open-mindedly."

But try as we would, our discussions always turned into noisy arguments, on five days of the week. But not on weekends, for Dad came home then, and *he* was the law. We didn't argue with *him*—we *discussed*.

He was a man to respect. He was dignified, clean, neat, and tidy at all times, and looked quite out of character in old work clothes, which he donned whenever possible to "carpenter" or "paint." He did all things *well*. "There's no sense in shoddy work," was his oft-repeated admonition to us. "It takes just as much effort and just as much time to do a bad job as it does to do a good job."

Came spring, and the "gleam" appeared in Dad's eyes. The first balmy day found him taking his yearly walk outside, going thrice around the house. Once again, he had the "housepainter's itch," and the boys groaned.

"Ach du liefer," grumbled Andy in his own version of Pennsylvania Dutch, which neither he nor any of us could speak but would take a stab at during times of stress or strain. "He gets the itch, and *we* have to paint."

So to the hardware store Dad would go to stock up on every conceivable tool and, of course, paint—buckets and buckets of the stuff. He would buy brushes enough to go around and some to spare, in case any of our friends were foolish enough to volunteer their help, wire brushes, sandpaper (from the heavy to very fine grain), primer, and enough turpentine to blow up a battleship.

"But," as Jonnie said dryly, "it's just our luck to live inland." He stared into space. "That would be fun," he said dreamily, "use up the stuff by blowing up a battleship." His eyes glittered for a long while with this thought.

Dad was filled with a sense of well-being—a homeowner's pride in the knowledge that *his* house was about to become the neatest, cleanest, and most shining abode in the block. His steps actually became light and jaunty, even as his eyes gleamed in anticipation.

"We begin on June 1," he announced to the table at large. It was then May 25, and we all were cramming like mad to pass our end-of-the-year exams in the highest possible standing, to which Dad and Muzzie had accustomed us, and we were looking forward to summer vacation. Ah, the loafing, sleeping late, swimming, tennis, etc., etc., were all a dream. Now he tells us that the paint job was to begin even before school was over. Only rain could deliver us.

"Huh," Jonnie snorted as he glared at me. "Why are *you* groaning? You're a *girl*. You don't have to get out there and paint!"

"Maybe I don't paint," I admitted, "but I have all the mess to clean up! Did you ever have all the paint brushes to clean, all the spots to mop and scrub up, and…?"

"Okay, okay," Jonnie growled. "So you're overworked."

The painting began. Dad was happy and particular! He, Bob, Andy, John, and Jim wielded the brushes.

On the second day of painting, Winnie, riding a borrowed bicycle down the street, streaked by screaming at the top of her lungs, "Help! Help! I can't stop it! Save me!"

Jim slid down the ladder, straddling the sides, and *leaped* down the street, catching the runaway bike just as it reached the intersection. He ran so fast that it is doubtful that his feet hit the concrete. He held his kid sister gruffly as she sobbed on his shoulder and advised, "Okay now, stop your blubbering and blow your nose. You don't want Muzzy to see you like this."

By that time, we were all gathered around, and each of us took a turn at hugging and comforting her. But her spasmodic sobbing only let up when Muzzy held her.

Our house was described to perfection only once that I can recall. George did it when only in the first grade, and I've often wondered how the idea had escaped the rest of us all those years before.

George's teacher was holding a quiz on types of materials used in building homes, and she'd received a good variety of answers. The class had slowed to a halt, and she urged them on. "All right Betty, tell us what kind of house you have?"

"Brick," said Betty.

"Davey, what kind have you?"

"Oh, wood, I guess," he replied.

"George, what kind of house do you have?"

George had been unusually thoughtful as the others took their turns, and when the teacher came to him, he said very seriously "I think our house is made of rubber."

"Why do you say that, George?" The teacher was trying to keep a straight face.

"Because I heard my big brother say it *stretches!*"

Dad and the boys finished the attic and made a boys' dormitory. They painted the outside of the house, built upstairs and downstairs closets, added to the dining room and finished the cellar. Every improvement helped in coping with our brood, and was *much* appreciated by we who lived within its bulging walls.

Muzzy had two favorite bushes, the mock orange and the lilac, and no doubt they *were* her favorites. Certainly they were her only bushes. They alone were sturdy enough to withstand the daily assault of her eleven children.

One stood in each of the far corners of our backyard, but it seemed to me that they had a "huddled" look about them, as though they were trying almost desperately to avoid something—a guided missile, perhaps, in the shape of a bike or wagon or tricycle, a baseball or bat or, in football season, a miscalculated flying tackle.

But they bloomed, each in its own season, and each with its own inimitable fragrance that we all, despite our noisy exuberance and seeming lack of interest in the "finer things of life," inhaled with deep and long-held breaths.

Five backyards down from ours, neatly fenced in and constantly under the loving, watchful eye of its owner Mr. Swengle, was a magnificent oxheart cherry tree. In the spring, the fragrance of the blossoms filled the neighborhood air with a haunting perfume—a promise of even better things to come. In the summer, the tiny, flat, green seeds grew and grew, and the summer sun and rain ripened them into a dark ruby lusciousness, each cherry a mouth-watering succulent delight to behold.

As the tree became more and more full of dark-ruby orbs, the birds arrived. In steady streams they came, and although Mr. Swengle waved his arms and shouted to frighten them off, it was to no avail. But the neighborhood boys were ready. Out came the slingshots, and in lieu of one of these weapons, a good pitching arm got more practice. Those black oxheart beauties were definitely *not* for the birds.

But it was a sure thing that Mr. Swengle didn't get all the cherries on his tree, not nearly all. For during the late evening hours, the tree shook with mysterious tremors. There was no breeze to shake it, but many boys slithering and slipping among its branches were reason enough for the trees' agitation. Muzzie paid Mr. Swengle for many a box of oxheart cherries that she never saw, much less tasted. Golly they were good!

At our house, there was a never-ceasing pitter-patter of eleven pairs of feet ranging in size from tiny baby booties to size 12 clodhoppers, and the volume of sound was commensurate with the size of each foot.

Upstairs and downstairs, through the house, in and out of the house, raced the feet, topped with long legs, sturdy bodies, well-balanced heads, through all of which ran an overwhelming exuberance for life.

Small wonder then that Muzzie, beaten and battered by the constant nerve-wracking, ceaseless noises about her was wont to cry out almost hopelessly, but not without her usual flash of humor, "*Please*, slam the door *softly!*"

Dad decided nine years after we moved into our house that he'd refinish the steps leading to the second floor. He got all of his equipment together and cleared everyone out. "No traffic for a while. Everybody use the bathroom and then skedaddle!"

He removed the rubber stair pads and asked me to run the cleaner over the stairs, after which he'd sand and I could run it again. I ran the cleaner, and he went to the kitchen for a glass of water.

He returned and idly watched me clean. Suddenly his eyes got big and his mouth dropped open. "Wha…a…a…t in the world! I don't believe it!" He closed his eyes tightly and then looked again at the stairs. "Carrie, lo…o…o…k!.

The center of each stair tread was worn off as though carved to make a deep, rounded seat. Carved by many feet, the off treads were more worn than the even ones because the boys always skipped steps.

He went downtown, bought new treads, and finished the job.

We had wonderful Halloween parties to keep us in the house on that night. Muzzie dressed up along with the rest of us, and each of us was allowed to invite four friends. Big families seldom have big houses, and we were no exception. We really bulged on that night of the year! We played musical chairs and bobbed for apples and had table loads of refreshments. Muzzie had as much fun and laughed as much as the rest of us.

Uninvited kids Halloweening in the area gave us a good dose of tricks, but the boys were ready for them. Jonnie stood on the front porch roof with a bucket of water and Jimmie on the back porch roof with another bucket of water, guarding the freezer of homemade ice cream on the back porch. The screams that occurred as the trickers were dunked were not heard indoors because of all of the noisy games, and Muzzie never knew what went on outside.

We had no great acres of land to play on, only a tiny bit in front of the house and a little bigger tiny bit in back. But we had an open field across the street, and far beyond that, we had a series of hills and dales called the bird sanctuary. This often became ours too when we knew there was much work to be done at home. The only trouble was that we all knew about the place and the caves along the bluff, so naturally we knew where to look for the culprit when Muzzie sent us out for him.

The bluff was our sanctuary, our hideout, our meeting place for the "gang."

Looking down from above, the cliff and rocky ledges below looked almost like a sheer drop of at least a thousand feet, well, a hundred feet, and there was a path very narrow and hard to find at first. Below, and running along the base of the cliff, was a small stream named Coal Creek. On either side of the "crick" was a narrow piece of flat land. It was an eerie spot because the sunlight could barely filter through the trees that rose almost as high as the bluff itself, and each fall sent a carpet of leaves and evergreen needles down to cover it so that no footfall could ever be heard.

Here we spent happy hours in groups or alone, depending on our courage. Here too we came with our hurts or heartbreak of the moment so that we could cry or fight it out alone. Here we played cops and robbers and cowboys and indians, gathered hickory nuts in the fall and elderberries for jelly. Here was our place to howl without disturbing anyone, and sometimes without an audience.

I remember putting on my own performance as a movie actress without an audience, playing the part of an Indian princess, standing on the very top of the bluff and singing with the greatest feeling, and volume, "The Indian Love Call."

I'd reached the second chorus and, with gestures, was singing, "When I'm calling you…oo…oo…ooo…ooo…oo…oooooo!" At that most beautiful moment—when I knew that no one would ever turn me down for the leading part in a fabulous opera—a young man, nicely dressed and carrying a suitcase, came up the path from below, grinning from ear to ear!

I stopped right in the middle of my "*ooooo*'s," mouth open in shock, turned, and ran as fast as I could back home.

I never even tried to find out who he was or why he was there—and with a suitcase!

Across the creek was forbidden territory (private property) and was an enticingly beautiful spot. To get across the creek was a simple matter, as long as you knew how to swing on the monkey vines. We screamed with delight if we made it across or with anguish if we missed and landed in the coal-dirt-filled waters.

Sympathy and concern were freely given by those looking on, mainly for the whaling the culprit would get at home when he or she came in with coal dirt in their clothing

"Take it like this," my younger brother Jonnie instructed me on my first try. He gripped the vine high up with one hand and a little lower with the other, walked back a short distance, took a running start, and, exactly at the creek's edge, lifted his feet and swung across the water, landing on a nice grassy slope on the other side.

"Now," he called, throwing the vine back at me, "you try it."

I gulped, but it *had* looked easy, so I was game. I gripped properly, walked back a short distance, took a running start, and kept on running—right into the water.

"Oh, you dumbbell!" he yelled. "Why didn't ya lift your feet?"

Having a load of coal dirt and water in both socks and shoes, I felt no need for conversation.

"Boy, you're gonna get it!" he yelled, adding fuel to the coal dirt. I knew that I was going to "get it," but I wasn't as worried about that as about my shoes.

At our house, shoes were important. When any of us needed shoes, Muzzie sent us down to Endicott Johnson's, and Mr. Smith, the manager, fitted us properly. He knew what we wanted because Muzzie had told him on the phone. It did no good whatsoever to try to wrangle another kind of shoe of our choice from Mr. Smith. He and Dad and Muzzie had an understanding. And too, Dad always paid a huge shoe bill at the beginning of each month. Oxfords we got, and oxfords we wore. Each of us had three pairs: one pair for Sunday school, one pair for school, and one pair for play. Seldom was there enough left of a pair of shoes to hand down, so each new pair must fit properly with "room to grow." And we were expected to take care of them too!

The waterlogged, coal-dirtied shoes scrunched accusingly at me as I made for the nearest log. True, they were only my play shoes, but they were *shoes* nevertheless. Jonnie glided effortlessly back to my side of the creek and, for once, proved smarter than I thought. He kept quiet.

With difficulty, I pulled off the oxfords and the once-pink but now-black socks. They were easy enough to wring out and then shake out most of the tiny coal flakes, but the color was still almost black. But how to wring out shoes?

First, I shook them. A few bits of coal dirt flew about, along with some drops of water, but that was all. I took two long sticks, put one shoe on the end of each, and tried to wave them to and fro to hurry the air-drying process, but that was too cumbersome. Johnnie obligingly took over one of the sticks. However, Jonnie, always the energetic one, whooshed the stick so fast that the shoe shot off the end and landed, yes, of course, in the creek.

I was given the lead in a school operetta, and while I was thrilled with the great honor, I was also petrified. On the evening of the performance, with Dad and Muzzie in the audience, I sang a duet with another performer. I could see Dad with a big grin on his face the whole time, which puzzled me.

After the show, Muzzie commented, "Two beautiful youngsters, and you sang so *well*." Dad had a different opinion. "Like two zombies. You were supposed to be *happy* when you sang the duet. I nearly cracked my face smiling so you'd see and smile too."

Our living room was much lived in, but some things were special: Dad's chair, Muzzie's chair, the books in the glass-doored bookcase, and, of course, the bookcase itself. Woe unto anyone who broke one of the glass doors! And woe unto anyone who mistreated a book! The davenport and the two matching overstuffed chairs were covered with a brown material that was very soft, almost velvety, to the touch, and they were to be *sat* on—carefully. Any rough stuff meant the *floor*.

Here too were the table lamps with varicolored glass shades somewhat like stained glass windows, and two floor lamps each with a three-inch fringe at the base of the shade. The table lamp sat in the very center of a long table which we called "The Library Table." This, no doubt, was because there were small shelves from the floor to the table surface at each end, backed by another pair of legs, and a long shelf from end-to-end near the floor. It made a lovely foot-rest–but only if no one was looking.

On the table were several stacks of magazines arranged very neatly, including the most special stack, the never-to-be-touched-with-sticky-fingers stack, which was made up solely of the *National Geographic Magazines* These were evidently meant for posterity, for never were we allowed to cut out even one little picture, even though our schoolwork of the moment just cried out for those special subjects.

To be able to sit around the library table to study meant we were "one of the bigger ones." It was an honor. And besides, no "bigger one" would be guilty of idly digging into that sacred tabletop with a pencil while thinking out a problem. Personally, I much preferred the big oval kitchen table with its oil-cloth cover, wiped clean after the evening meal and ready to receive its many columns of addition and subtraction for, if written lightly enough, an eraser would quickly destroy all evidence.

We had good books in our home and read them all. We were always buried in a book, and when Muzzie needed us, she called three or four times before we even heard her.

She too loved to read but seldom had time for it. If she sat down without some work to occupy her hands, there was at least one, usually two, little ones to climb on her lap to be held and rocked.

I once cut the back of my hand and forgot about it until it began to swell and give me pain. Finally, a few days after the cut, Muzzie caught sight of it and was shocked. The hand was at least twice its normal size.

"Oh, Marney. How could you let it get so bad! Bob, take her to Dr. Thomas right away!"

She telephoned the good, patient, long-suffering doctor, and he was waiting for us.

He tut-tutted a bit and then got busy. "Hold tight to her, Bob. Turn your head away, Marney. This will hurt."

Bob held me so that I couldn't pull my hand away. I turned my head. It *did* hurt. He sliced into the infection and drained and drained and drained and drained.

Even Bob was white around the gills on that one. I felt a great relief from one pain, although it was replaced by a new one. More than anything, I needed to vomit, and I did.

With shaking fingers, I held the phone while the operator connected us. "Oh, Dr. Thomas…Noonie fell down the attic stairs and cracked his head open…and it's bleeding all over the place…Mother's holding it together. Can you come, *please?*"

The quiet voice on the other end of the line asked no questions. "Right away, Marney," he said, and the calm of his tone was a haven of hope to me.

It wasn't until afterward—when he'd stitched up the wound on poor Noonie's forehead, made a little joke and turned our fears into smiles, and had left—that I realized I hadn't told him on the phone *who* I was. Somehow he had known.

The boys decided they needed to tone their muscles, so they rigged up a chinning bar in the upstairs hallway. This, of course, was done despite the fact that with only one bathroom in the house, the hall was used almost as much as Grand Central Station.

They made one concession to the safety and/or prevention of cracked skulls by putting signs up on the wall beside the stairs. The first one read, "Careful! Duck!" The second, a bit more terse and a little farther up the stairs, read, "Duck!" The third and last was just beyond the place where the chinning bar was fastened and said simply, "Too Bad!"

Tom was the one who could handle money. Boy, could he handle it and handle it and handle it and then put it safely back in his bank. We would watch enviously as the stock of pennies, nickels, and dimes grew, and we would think, *Darn, can't he ever, just once, buy some candy with it?* We'd gladly have followed him to the store and watched that he didn't get cheated. And certainly, with our superior knowledge, we could show him the best buys, but for some reason, he never asked for our help.

We took easily to the new gadget called the telephone, and in the early years of its possession, on the rare occasions when it rang imperiously for attention, there was a wild scramble to be the first to answer it. We were given strict orders by Dad not to talk more than five minutes and *never* after nine o'clock at night.

"Anyway," he reminded us, "you should all be in bed by that time." After 9:00 p.m., he would want to call home and "talk to his girl," he said. He and Muzzy were still, as we teased them, pretty mushy about each other.

All went well with the phone until one weekend when Dad was home. The telephone rang. We didn't know that Dad was expecting an important business call, so the usual scramble ensued, and Andy won out. "Hello, he called into the thing. "This end's ready, are you?"

By that time, Dad had grabbed the receiver and glared us all into a quick fade-out. We didn't materialize again until hours later and only because we were hungry. We got it that time. He discovered that we'd all been answering the phone in like manner, or worse, and then and there laid down strict laws on "telephone manners!"

I awoke one morning with a sense of excitement. Just lying there in the deep feather mattress, I felt it. No, I smelled it. I couldn't decide at first what it was, and then I knew. It was the tiniest, almost imperceptible, fragrance. I shot up in bed. "It's spring!"

My big sister Bea, already up and nearly dressed, turned from the mirror, hairbrush held between strokes on her long chestnut hair, and grinned. "You noticed?" She breathed deeply and turned again to the mirror, hairbrush moving faster than before. "Then come on, sleepyhead. Get dressed. We're going out to pick dandelion."

"Dandelion?" I wailed. "Oh no!"

I hated the stuff, but Muzzie insisted we must have a good "cleaning out," and cooked dandelion was one of the best "cleaner outers" ever known, so she said. "Or," she would gaze directly at the one who turned up his nose at the dish, "you may have a choice—dandelion or sulfur and molasses." There was no more hesitation. Dandelion was much the lesser of the two evils, and you could chew it fast and swallow it, losing the taste forever when followed by a big slice of jelly bread. Sulfur and molasses, on the other hand, could be tasted and retasted for days after swallowing and was an experience to be endured once and only once.

"Okay." I scrambled out of bed. "I'm ready."

Bea, now busily braiding her hair into two thick pigtails, grinned at me in the mirror. I reached for the pile of clothes on the chair beside the bed, slipping out of my long flannel nightgown and into the short-sleeved undershirt, and then backed up to Bea to button my pantywaist up the back, then into my black bloomers. I tried not to look as I stepped into them, for I hated and despised them with all of my being. However, since Muzzie made all of our clothes, I had no choice.

"Your everyday bloomers will be black until you are a young lady and no longer a tomboy," she said.

I remember suggesting that "Bea is still a tomboy, but she gets to wear white panties." At that Mother had sighed and shook her head. "Never mind, Marney. Just never mind." I thought at the time how unfair it was, but I didn't fuss. I'm sure there was a hint of sympathy in Muzzie's eyes, which she didn't dare voice, and I felt a bit closer to her for the moment. And after all she *was* right. Rolling around on the ground, battling any one of my brothers who disagreed with me, down on my knees in the dust shooting marbles with the boys, playing kick-the-ricket or baseball or football, always with the boys, was I guess "being a tomboy."

I used to box with my brothers, but I hated to be hit in the face. So I would either turn my back on my opponent and strike out backward or get in close to him, hitting the air in front of his face with both hands waving fast and furiously. This always got them. They could do nothing but double over, helpless with laughter.

"Marney," Bea urged as she left the room, "stop dreaming and hurry."

I jumped and pulled up the long black cotton-ribbed stockings, fastened them to my pantywaist garters, then the cotton petticoat and overall, an old blouse and jumper (dark green this time so as not to show the dirt), and my oldest shoes, black button type just above my ankles. I was ready. I started downstairs, turned back to grab my brush and made several strokes at my hair, and raced down the stairs.

There was the smell of pancakes this morning and fresh brewed coffee (for grownups only, but I loved the smell) and the deeper, smoother fragrance of rising bread dough. Chairs were already scraping as the family gathered around the big kitchen table, and I slid into my place just in time to fold my hands and bow my head for Dad's prayer.

It was a good prayer. He made them up differently each time, and I wondered again how he knew what to talk about to God. But he never hesitated, and he didn't make them too long, either, not like the minister when he came to dinner. On one of those occasions, Andy had whispered to me during the minister's prayer (and got his bottom whacked later), "If he doesn't soon say 'Amen,' I'll fall over from hunger." I'd kicked his ankle for that because I thought I should, but inwardly I agreed with him. Thereafter, when the minister was to appear, we always tried to snitch a piece of bread or a bit of meat before dinner to hold us through that prayer.

I'm always surprised that our babies grew up unscathed and unmutilated. Perhaps it was because we older ones had to look after the younger ones or, more likely, it was in spite of that fact.

Noonie was in the carriage on the sidewalk in my care one day when a group of neighborhood kids came outside to shoot their bows and arrows. Unfortunately, they shot them up into the air, and one came down straight at the carriage. I leaned over the baby to shield him, but the blunt-pointed arrow zoomed past my shoulder and hit Noonie above his eyebrow. He was okay, in spite of his loud howls, but the shooter was severely punished by his parents for that little stunt.

As each baby came, we loved it, and as he or she grew older, we bossed it as we had been loved and bossed. We fought with each other, but let any outsider dare to ever say anything against one of our own and we pitched in to do battle royale.

Often, had we dared, we'd have sent a half dozen or so of the younger ones to an orphanage just to get some peace and solitude. Naturally, we'd have gotten them out of hock before nightfall, but, no doubt, only because of our nightly nose count.

"If we didn't have so darn many kids,'" one of us would growl.

Then Muzzie would ask, "Which of them would you give up?" That always stopped us.

Each of us older ones was responsible for a younger one no matter where we were, so we developed an ultra sense of responsibility. If we went on picnics, our "sense" would tell us a younger one was straying beyond the limits or had shinnied up a tree and couldn't get down but was yet undecided about whether to advertise the fact by screaming for help. If we went swimming, our sense told us how many were in the water and at which exact location as well as how many times Jonnie had gone under just to test our sense.

To and from Sunday school and church, at football and basketball games, playing kick-the-ricket down at the corner or on a treasure hunt, the sense was constantly at work. Sometimes it was a real pain in the neck and often brought groans from us older ones.

The older ones were constantly nagging the younger ones.
"Tie your shoe laces."
"Why didn't you polish them?"
"Button your coat."
"Comb your hair."
"Did you brush your teeth?"

"You have a button off."

"Press your skirt or trousers."

Cleanliness Is Next to Godliness was our home rule and was passed on down through the ranks.

Being the fifth child in a family of eleven children wasn't so bad. The half-forbidden things, like wearing lipstick and nail polish, were already battled over and ironed out by the two older girls, and it was smooth-sailing go-ahead for me. And being the fifth child, third daughter, down the line gave me a lovely anonymity, a sort of free-as-a-bird status because I was actually buried among the rest.

However, it had its drawbacks. I was appointed, or automatically accepted, the job of chief custodian to the little ones, and only on rare moments of their waking hours was I free of them. Anyway, when Muzzie called, I obeyed.

"Marney, please change the baby's diapers." (I became a proficient diaper changer.)

"Marney. Please take Tommy to room #7 before you go to bed. And Winnie and Noonie too," she added as an afterthought.

This became a nightly ritual, and believe me, trying to dehydrate *three* (one at a time, of course) sleep-befogged, limp, snuggly little bodies in the middle of the night is not easy. They lean on you and would fall flat on their faces if you didn't prop them up. And, of course, they didn't know what they were supposed to do. They would just sit there—sleeping.

Finally, dehydration accomplished, I would tuck Tommy back into his bed, George into his crib in my room, and Winnie into the bed with me. Then at last I could slip into bed and stretch out. It was only a moment before Winnie snuggled closer and slid first one leg and then the other across my stomach, and no amount of twisting and turning could dislodge them. And so we slept.

From our earliest years, each of us felt the deep need for privacy, that "aloneness" so impossible to find in a large family. If by some great fortune we found a nook or cranny unoccupied and—blessing of all blessings—*silence*, we were, without a doubt, in heaven!

I believe Jimmie was the only one among us who *truly* found privacy, even in the midst of all the turmoil, and he accomplished that so easily that it amazed me. All he did was sit down, usually on the floor, with the toy or book of the moment, look quite cheerful and happy, and *completely* ignore us. Of course, he was helped somewhat by the fact that he crawled under Muzzie's sewing machine, which stood in one corner of the kitchen, and played contentedly while sitting on the foot treadle. And the fact that a foot treadle will seat only one comfortably. This, no doubt, was the forerunner of the modern playpen.

Dad gave Muzzie fifty-dollar-a-week household money, a fortune in those days, and she needed every penny of it. The baker left nine loaves of bread every Saturday and three on weekdays.

Muzzie loved to go to market. Twice a week in the winter and three times a week in the summer she went, starting early so that she would have a choice of the freshest fruits and vegetables. She carried the big basket over her arm, and one of the younger boys followed with the boys' coaster wagon. When her basket grew heavy, she put it in the wagon and finished the job with the smaller basket that was still in the wagon.

She was a marvelous cook and delighted in preparing good meals. One of our favorites was pork tenderloin, a long piece of the very best meat sliced and fried. But anything that Muzzie made was always mouth-watering, absolutely perfect! Her roast beef was tender beyond belief. Her vegetable soup accompanied by her freshly baked biscuits and home-canned fruit was worth *running* home to, especially on a cold winter evening. Her baked goods of every kind were so delicious that they rarely lasted another day. Her pies were all flaky and tender—Montgomery, shoofly, crumb, peach, apple, cherry, and huckleberry. We were johnny-on-the-spot on "doughnut day" and for her cookies of every shape, size, and flavor. It was a rare day when one of her baked concoctions was a failure and a day of mourning for all of us. We walked softly with long faces in sympathy and never, never mentioned the subject.

We all gathered berries for the pies, spreading out over the countryside and filling our baskets to the top (with a few for eating along the way). Later, when we returned home, we cleaned and washed them so that they were ready for the huge canning kettle.

The 7:30 p.m. fire whistle was our warning to "head for home,'" and during vacation in the summer, the 9:00 p.m. curfew meant all children get *home*! And if we weren't, there was a great "hallooing" from parents on front porches all up and down the street!

Our summer rainy-day hangouts were our big front porches where we played jacks or, in the evenings, told ghost stories, played "My Father Owned a Grocery Store," and sang songs, some sitting on the porch swing, some on banisters, and some on the steps.

On nice hot rainy days, without thunder and lightning, the preschool children donned bathing suits or old underwear (always of heavy cotton non-see-through) and ran around in the rain, up and down the pavements and in the gutters and made dams, so they really had something *deep* to splash in.

A *big treat* was a homemade freezer of ice cream. All the neighborhood kids came for that!

Monopoly had just come out and was so popular that it was sold out in most places. One bitter cold evening, when sleet and rain had left a sheet of ice over everything, I slipped and slid all the way to the Third and Market Street Rea & Derrick Drugstore where I found their one last set. Was I a *hero* when I returned home! That evening was the first of many marathon games.

We grew and grew and grew, and nothing gave more clear testimony to that fact than the let-down dress hems and pant cuffs.

"The dresses are easy," Muzzie always claimed. "I can cover the old hem mark on the dress with a row of rickrack. But"—she frowned worriedly—"a pair of pants?" She sighed.

I offered the obvious solution. "How about a lace ruffle added to the bottom?"

The boys looked at me with distaste, muttering, "Pretty funny."

We jealously guarded the oldest ones' clothes, knowing that they'd be passed down to us someday. Woe unto them if they treated a garment with a lack of respect.

Muzzie was always washing and ironing, for in the years after we all arrived, there were fifty to sixty shirts to iron every week besides everything else. She made most of the girls' clothing and some for the boys. The old treadle sewing machine was always piled high with mending or a new sewing project. When she was expecting another baby, one of us treadled for her until Dad had an electric motor connected to it, and then the old machine really whirred.

On wash day, we turned the crank on a remarkable new washing machine. The scrubbing board was put aside but never discarded because we had too many *really* dirty knees. The wringer turned too, by golly—no more wringing by hand. We took turns, and the result was line upon line of clean clothes. So many that there was no room for playing in the yard on wash day.

There were always two ironing boards set up on ironing day, Tuesday. Muzzie took one, while the other was used by anyone who was there at the moment. Before my turn, they used flat irons, heated on the big black cookstove, two at a time and two spares kept hot while the first two were being used.

By the time I was old enough to man the second ironing board at about age seven, doing the flat pieces, we had graduated to electric irons. They were heavy and clumsy and plugged into the electric light cord that dangled from the ceiling, but they were, oh my, *so* convenient!

One day we came home from school to find the big old black cookstove gone and a beautiful white and black gas stove in its place. We loved it, but Muzzie was wary of it for many months, even though she had to use it for feeding her hungry mob.

Shortly after that, Dad had central heating put in. A big new coal furnace took up residence in the cellar, and the sitting room stove was also removed.

"This is living!" Bob and Andy decided, even though they still shoveled coal onto the fire and dug ashes from the ash pit.

One winter day, Muzzie was sick with a very bad cold. She had done the laundry, and it was all ready to be hung out, and lunch was nearly ready when she had to go to bed. Bob and Andy, with two of their football-player friends, Scotty and Russ who had been invited several days before, arrived along with all of us.

Muzzie sick? I ran upstairs to check on her and came back and took firm charge.

"Okay, you fellas. Grab the two baskets of laundry in the cellar and the clothespins and hang out the wash!"

All four of them began hanging the laundry on the backyard clothes line.

"Throw me some nails," they called, and several clothespins flew through the air at a time, to be caught in their hands.

"Everyone wash your hands and eat, so we can wash the dishes and clean up before we go back to school. *Dapeche vous* [hurry]!" I was taking French in school and already bore signs of a great "top sergeant."

We rammed lunch into our mouths as I took the dishes away from everyone to wash and dry, and then we chased the little ones back to their school and raced to ours a mile away. I didn't run; they lifted me off my feet. All this in one hour!

Muzzie's family was her life. Her love was equally distributed, and she always had more for the next new baby.

SLAM THE DOOR SOFTLY

But she had no favorites, and she was always fair and just with her decisions and/or punishments.

One of our happiest sights coming home from school in the spring or fall was seeing Muzzie sitting on a rocker on the front porch, sewing or mending. She looked so neat and clean and rested and was, for a change, not down on her knees scrubbing or standing over a hot ironing board.

She was a very active PTA member and always had a very reasonable explanation when anyone asked incredulously, "How do you ever get the time to attend the meetings and do so much PTA work?"

"I really enjoy the meetings," she'd reply. "And I like working with the other mothers." Then she'd smile and add, "With *my* family, I could hardly stay away." Her responsibilities were hers, and she assumed them.

She was invited by the PTA to write a paper on how to raise a family. At first, she had no idea what to say, but then just wrote about how we all had duties and had to help each other. Everyone loved it.

The teachers liked her. They could always depend on her to chastise us properly if we misbehaved at school. "After all," Muzzie reminded us sternly, "Your teachers are there to *teach* and not to make you *behave*," and always, "You go to school to *learn*. Now see that you *do*."

We had one old grouch of a teacher who was worn and worried nearly to death by her ailing parents. Because she was unable to relax and smile in school, she was bedeviled by the troublemakers until she was at her wit's end. My brother John was one of those boys.

One day Miss B. went out of the class room for no more than five minutes and returned to find John's seat empty. "Where is John Snyder?" she asked.

No one answered, but one by one the pupils looked up at the ceiling, drawing her eyes upward too.

There was John. He had shinnied up the center pole in the room and was nonchalantly hanging on, grinning down at everyone.

"John Snyder!" she shouted. "You get down here this minute and take your seat!"

He obediently slid down the pole and sat at his desk, while Miss B. gave him a long angry lecture. Then she turned to the blackboard and wrote his name in its usual place, heading the "Stay in After School" list. "Punishment will be drastic this time," she muttered.

John, in the meantime, was leaning over and very quietly loosening the screws that fastened the desk to the floor. When she turned around, she got quite a shock!

There stood John, desk lifted off the floor, asking innocently, "Where shall I take it, Miss B?"

He was expelled and went to the bluff, afraid to go home.

I walked home, not fast, trying to figure out what and how to tell Muzzie about John's latest escapade and how to soften it. If only Bob and Andy would come home soon, I could waylay them, but they'd be at football practice,

Jimmy came up behind me. "Hi, Marney, hey, don't you feel good?" he asked.

"No, I'm thinking."

"Is that why?"

Still deep in thought, I said, "Why what?"

"Why you don't feel good?" He was only asking.

SLAM THE DOOR SOFTLY

But my problem was unresolved, and I couldn't shield John. I'd have to tell Muzzie, and he'd never come home.

John finally showed up in time for supper and confessed his misdeeds to Muzzie. She worded his apology to the teacher, and he recited it the next day. He must have seemed genuinely contrite because he was forgiven.

Muzzie's pull taffy was something so luscious, so completely melt-in-the-mouth, that it was easy to drool at the mere thought of it. Only she could cook the syrup to the proper consistency, and only she could pull it with the delicate fingertip touch needed to bring it to perfection. She stood on the back porch where the cool fall breezes would make it just right, arms aching and chilled to the bone, and we all stood about too, freezing. But it smelled so good that we didn't mind in the least.

It was an art and she the artist, and we weren't alone in that knowledge. Much to our chagrin, she always shared with friends and neighbors. Worst of all we had to be honorable and carry, intact, the basket or box of goodies next door or down the street or halfway across town. It's easiest to be honorable when you only have to go next door!

Our teachers loved Muzzie's pull taffy. So did our friends and classmates, but they never had a chance on Bake Sale Days at school.

When a PTA bake sale was scheduled one of the teachers would always come up to me before school was over and ask, "Marney, do you think your mother will have time to make some of her delicious pull taffy for the sale?"

And I, of course, feeling very important, would dare only say, "I think she might. I'll ask her."

That was all Muzzie needed. A request for something that others thought *she* could do best! She dropped everything to do it.

But there was no use telling the other kids about it. Long ago, at one of the bake sales, they had had a chance to buy a piece or two and had loved it. But no more! The teachers loved it too and bought it up before we were let out for recess when we were allowed to buy our goodies.

The upright piano in our living room should, by all rights, have been the first instrument used by eleven great composers. It was on this old Vough that each of us played our greatest masterpieces, always composed of great peals of lightning and mighty crashes of thunder that accompanied our own vocal renditions of heartbreakingly beautiful trills and garbled words. It isn't easy to sit alone at the piano in a six-room house with twelve other people in it, but we took it for granted that it was fair and proper for the other fellow to have a turn at the upright and kept clear of that immediate area until the "genius" had finished his masterpiece.

I can't remember when the upright didn't have the place of honor in our house. It had been bought with care, and even though it was second-hand, Dad was fussy in choosing the best. Muzzie was thrilled. Mary always felt that it was hers and that she had first crack at the piano. She took pride in keeping it polished and the keys beautifully white. She discovered one day that the piano keys had three nicks in them, probably because someone had dropped something and chipped them. However, she swore that one of us had bitten the keys and caused the jagged edges. She forcibly brought each of us to the piano and made us bare our teeth to see whose front ones matched the nicks.

Because of Muzzie's great singing talent, most of us had inherited fairly good singing voices, and the upright learned to play many kinds of music, hymns at first and some of the good old classics—"Mother Machree," "Whispering Hope," etc. But these sounded best if Muzzie sang them alone. We never were more quiet than on these lovely rare occasions.

Two weeks until Christmas and all through the house the Snyder's were rushing–all eleven of us children and Muzzie and Dad weren't sitting idle, either. This was happiness time, so excruciatingly exciting that it was impossible to calm down.

Mary, home from nursing school, and Bea and Bob, home from college, were lucky enough to get holiday jobs and were downtown in the thick of it, rushing home for meals and then back to those salesclerk and stock-boy jobs.

Andy and the younger boys had already harvested the hickory nuts from that special group of trees in the woods known only to the family. They had brought them home in the sturdy flour sacks that Muzzie kept laundered and ready for any and every use—even to the bodices she made for the little ones, to which she attached the long garters to hold up their black cotton stockings.

Just one week ago, on schedule, Andy, John and Jim brought out the old flat irons, those without handles, and several hammers. Then carefully spreading newspapers on the kitchen table and a "Christmas goody" tablecloth over that, they went to work.

Andy, being the oldest of that group, laid down the laws: "Hit the *nut* with the hammer, not your finger." This brought giggles from the little ones gathered around to watch, marvel, and snitch any stray or flying nuts. "No," he corrected Jimmy. "Don't put the nut on the table to crack it. Lay it on the flat iron, hold it steady, and then hit it with the hammer."

"Hey, what's the matter with this one?" asked Tommy, pointing out an exceptionally large, round, and prickly "something" that was dumped from one of the bags along with the hickory nuts.

"That's the outer shell," Andy explained patiently. "That must come off first, carefully, those stickers hurt! Just hit it hard, and the shell cracks open. There now, it'll come off." He looked around at each pair of interested eyes. "Now remember, these are for Muzzie to make Christmas *candies* and *cookies*! They're not for *you*"—he eyed each one sternly—"to eat *now*. Understood!"

There were more giggles and then a sheepish nodding of heads while at the same time passing nudges around the circle to indicate a willingness to snitch should the opportunity present itself.

Muzzie had been watching and enjoying the small playlet as she sat in her special sewing corner, safe from our prying eyes in this "forbidden area," finishing one of her Christmas surprises for one or the other of us. Now it was time for her intervention if there were to be any hickory nuts for her goodies.

"Now boys," she said. "Behave."

That was enough. They grinned at her to let her know that they'd only been fooling and hadn't *really* meant it. But she knew better and watched the proceedings with her own eyes twinkling but prepared.

The older ones who worked could really splurge, but for us younger ones, Muzzie and Dad gave each of us spending money (ten cents for each gift) and helped us plan our expedition to the 5 &10 Cent Store. She made it as exciting as a trip to Mars, whispering and returning a knowing smile at the proper time. The Salvation Army Santa, with his bell and kettle, stood in the snow outside the store, and the peals of his bell rang joyous Christmas music in the crisp air. After we had chosen the perfect presents, we sidled into the house and wrapped them with much whispering and giggling.

She made dozens and dozens of cookies and hid them so they would last until Christmas. We always snitched some along the way from the big can Muzzie "hid" so there would be plenty for Christmas because for eleven children, there were no hiding places! We shelled the walnuts that we had gathered in the fall for Muzzie to use for fudge, fondant, and cookies.

Muzzie loved Christmases and made it our best-loved memory. Her love of music was almost satisfied with the frequent gatherings around the piano to sing Christmas carols. We had begun to harmonize, and it was beautiful. Voices joined in from all parts of the house, and the rafters *really* rang.

We all trimmed the tree, placing much-loved ornaments upon it, and woe to the one who dropped any! Excitement mounted!

On Christmas morning, there was a sheet across the archway into the living room—no spying! "Eat a hearty breakfast," we were ordered, and then we were lined up, with the youngest "walking" child first followed by the rest of us in steps. Each Christmas a different one of us had one big gift and some small ones too. The rest had nice gifts too, chosen with *much* thought, but had to wait their turn for their big Christmas. It took a long time to come around to our second big Christmas.

One year, Bea and Bob pooled their money for a really big gift for the family. On Christmas morning, they stood on the stair landing and recited clues in poetry to us in the audience below. We finally figured it out—it was a commode seat!

Then there was running around to friends' houses to see their loot and they coming to our house to see ours. We didn't always get what we wanted, but we were always happy with what we did receive.

Birthdays were big too. Muzzie always made a cake, and we had gifts and much attention. We were never too crowded to include a few extra people in our celebration, and the house fairly bulged on Our Day.

Sophistication was the theme of the day. That, combined with Dad's constant reminder that "well-bred folk never show their feelings" and our family pretense of being descended from stoical Indians, inured us against any show of pain or emotion. Well, almost. We still shouted with laughter or with anger, but our pain we kept close to ourselves, sometimes bravely, but sometimes only because we were at a tender age when modesty was mixed with secretiveness.

One example of this was one night during supper when Muzzie noticed me only half-sitting on my chair.

"Sit straight, Marney," she directed. "You have a whole chair to yourself."

I pretended to move into proper position on my chair and began eating much faster than was normal for me.

But Muzzie was not satisfied. "Marney," she called above the clatter and din, "don't you feel well?"

"Oh sure, sure…I feel fine."

She eyed me narrowly, even as she rescued Noonie's baby dish, which he'd already lifted from his high chair tray and aimed toward Jimmy. "I want to see you after supper," she directed. "And *don't forget.*"

Well, a boil on one's posterior is never anything to boast about, but I was twelve, and at that tender, overmodest age when the thought of anyone—just *anyone*—seeing my bare bottom was unthinkable.

Muzzie took me to the bathroom, shut the door, prepared the proper bandages, and sterilized a needle.

"Marney!" Muzzie finally reached the point of exasperation. "I'm your *mother! Now you let me see that boil!*"

There was no hope of defying her when Muzzie spoke in that firm tone. Meekly and blushing violently, I bent over the chair, cautiously exposed the "spot," and Muzzie went to work. It hurt horribly, but I made no sound. Waiting only until the boil was lanced, drained, and bandaged to put my clothing straight again, I fled to the girls' room, tossing the expected but mumbled "Thanks" over my shoulder as I fled, stripped of all dignity and modesty.

Doing dishes was a necessary evil and endless. The designated "drier" or "dryers" always managed to slip away to room #7 just at the time he was needed, and the "washer" invariably set up a howl for Muzzie. Often she claimed it would be easier on her nerves if she did the dishes herself, but when she had corralled the drier and sent him to the kitchen, she could, at last, settle down to some peaceful darning of the mountainous pile of socks that awaited her.

We took our turns, but we didn't volunteer. For the sake of fairness, Muzzie was forced to make up a schedule for week, and she had to be a veritable Solomon in her choice.

"Mary, you wash this week. Marney and Jonnie dry, Bea and Jimmie, clear and crumb the table and put away the leftovers."

"But I washed all *last* week," Mary would cry. "That's not *fair*."

"Yes," Muzzie would agree. "But," she reminded her, "you got out of all the meal preparation because you were practicing for the school play and couldn't get home early last week, remember?"

Mary remembered. She objected no more and began urging the "clear-offers" to get moving so she could "get done before *midnight*."

Sometimes we had some jim-dandy arguments while washing and drying, but most of the time, we used this period for learning and teaching—the alphabet for the little ones who gathered at the big kitchen table and caroled along with us bigger ones, the multiplication tables for the middle-sized ones, algebra or geometry theorems for the oldsters. But at other times, the dishes were done in jig time as we sang rounds or made up our own words to popular music, such as "I'm Forever Blowing Bubbles." The song actually was,

> I'm forever blowing bubbles,
> Pretty bubbles in the air.
> They fly so high,
> Nearly reach the sky.

Our version was,

SLAM THE DOOR SOFTLY

> I'm forever washing dishes,
> Dirty dishes in the sink.
> They're piled so high,
> Nearly reach the sky,
> First I wash and then I dry.
> Mother's always scolding (Muzzie always winced here, but she knew we didn't mean it)
> I sit down and cry.
> I'm forever washing dishes,
> Dirty dishes in the sink-ee-ink-ee-ink.

Mary was operatically inclined, but she didn't know any opera, so she used the only material she had and sang the song for the first time with pathos, drama, and a tremolo in her voice while she idly swished at the dishwater. The boys waited until her last notes died away before adding their own finale. In unison, from all parts of the house, came the sound of a pack of hounds. Mary didn't appreciate their help and threatened horrible retribution if they didn't "cut that out!"

Bob and Andy took some of the sting out of it though when they began jazzing it up, and Mary could never again give the song her own full-blown tragic feelings. After hearing the new version several times, she added her voice to the others—at full volume. If she couldn't beat 'em, she might as well join 'em.

Sometimes the boys objected to doing "girls" work, but Muzzie reminded them, "We don't live on a farm, so there is no so-called boy's work to do. And since you live here too, you'll have to do your share of work—whether it's boy's work or not."

All of them learned to cook, wash and dry dishes, and clean. Some of them turned out pretty fancy baked goods too. The fact that they were rough and tough football players put the "quietus" on any taint of the name *sissy*.

Scrubbing the kitchen floor was a real project. Not only was it a backbreaking, time-consuming, knee-rawing experience, but it was also a matter of fine, almost hairbreadth, timing. After Bea went to college, it was my job—and I dreaded it.

It was supposed to be done on Saturday so it would be clean for any drop-in visitors on Sunday. So I would gather together all the paraphernalia and quiz the family individually. "When are you going out today? What time will you be back?" This was important. I had to do the job when traffic was at a minimum.

Tom would say, "I'm going to the market with Muzzie." (He'd be gone from eight to ten, then bring the marketing home in his wagon.)

"I'm going to the movies this afternoon."

"So am I."

"I'm going too."

Good! Three of them out of the way in one fell swoop. But they'd be gone from one to five, and darn it, I didn't want to be scrubbing a floor on Saturday afternoon.

Usually at about that point, I gave up. The heck with being nice and *asking* them. I'd *tell* them, "Okay, everyone, I'm scrubbing the floor from 8:00 to 10:00 a.m. Saturday morning. Make yourselves scarce. Get it!" They did, only because I was bigger than most of them, the older ones being away at school or at part-time jobs. They got!

It took scouring powder, of course, and plenty of elbow grease and bucket after bucket of water, but I was usually finished by 10:00 a.m.

Then the floor still not being completely dry, it was a good idea to spread newspapers as stepping stones for those who just *had* to come into the kitchen. And too, Muzzie would have to put away the groceries.

After this chore, I dragged my aching, dripping, and distinctly unglamorous body to the bathroom, hoping to catch a five-minute respite and soak in some *clean* water for a change. Andy, the bathroom "holdup," was inside and deep in a book. "Hurry up," I yelled. "I want a bath." Later, somewhat refreshed, I'd quit the bathroom, probably because someone was banging on the door.

In the meantime, the printed word had acted as a giant magnet to every member of the family. To see so much of it spread out over so huge an exposure as the kitchen floor, just waiting for each and every one of them to fall to and read the funnies (*Belinda, Hairbreadth Harry, Rudolph Rossendale, Orphan Annie,* and the *Katzenjammer Kids*), the news, sports—well, after all, the papers were at least two weeks old and people *do* forget. There they all were down on their knees, rumps upturned, leaning on elbows and completely absorbed.

Their upturned bottoms were a temptation, but no! *Let them stay in that other world for a while, I thought.* Then I gazed smugly at the clean floor underneath the readers and was satisfied.

Of course, Bob started it all. He was the oldest boy, and Dad wanted all of us to have everything he'd never had. Consequently, he wanted Bob to go out for football, which he did, and became one of the school's star players. He began it, and the other six boys followed suit.

With eleven children in our family, we had just enough for a football team, except for one drawback—four of us were *girls*. In those days, girls were not accepted by football coaches for a place on their teams, not even as bench warmers. So we girls did the next best thing and became cheerleaders, rooting our team on to victory come heck or high water and basking in reflected glory from the heroic efforts of our seven brothers in holding that line, blocking that kick, or (most glorious of all) making that touchdown.

Of course, they didn't all play at one time, being at least two years apart in age, and sometimes there was a leap of four years because one of us girls came in between. But they all played in their turn and kept the team pretty well stocked with quarterbacks for many a year.

During the "season," our table conversation just naturally became almost completely football, and we automatically ate, slept, and talked the game.

Bob, usually understanding and diplomatic, was a tarter in pointing out the younger boys' football "failures." At dinner, after one big game, Bob told Andy off. "You shoulda had that man, Andy," he said sadly, shaking his head reproachfully. "You were closer to him than anybody else, and you only had two of their guys tailing you."

"Whaddaya mean?" Andy was wide eyed and outraged at this accusation. "I was *closest* to him, yeah, but those two guys you say were *tailing* me were *riding my legs* and they were hanging on like *leeches!*"

Bea nodded emphatically. "He's right! I was standing right there where that play went on, and I saw it, just as he said." Being a cheerleader, and right on the side lines, she no doubt had, but Bob didn't take kindly to her remark.

"Humph!" He looked condescendingly at her, a little peeved because she was standing against him when she usually took his side on any issue. "Girls! What do they know about football?" He dropped that phase of his argument and went on to one of the other plays, this time tossing Andy a compliment—a rare and wonderful thing. "You did a nice job of blocking there in the third quarter."

That pleased everyone, and we relaxed again. No more need to take sides *this* meal.

But Bob hadn't finished. "Too bad it was one of *our* men you were blocking."

The football season was always an exciting time. But football itself was a worrisome game, and each year Muzzie had to prepare herself—"become hardened," she called it—for all of the injuries that went with the game.

One season, twice during practice and once during a game, Bob broke first his left collar bone, then his right collar bone, and then again his left collar bone. He was a *hero*, and we idolized him. But to Muzzie, he was her son and in pain. She deplored the game, worried constantly, and could only relax when, at the end of the day, all of her "chicks" were settled in bed. The first two broken bones were the hardest for her, and they were frightening to us too, perhaps because of the way we were informed.

We were helping to put dinner on the table about 5:30 p.m. when the phone rang.

"I'd like to speak to Mrs. Snyder please," said a deep, halting male voice.

Muzzie took the phone and heard the same voice speak, almost apologetically. "Mrs. S., this is Coach B. Your Bob was injured in practice a little while ago, and we have him here at the hospital." He gulped and took another deep breath. "Do you want to come over, ma'am?"

Muzzie's voice quavered, but she asked sensible questions. "Where is he hurt?"
"We think it's his shoulder."
"Is he thinking clearly?"
"Yes, ma'am. He's quite normal."
"Then he has no head injury?"
"No, ma'am."
"Are they taking x-rays?"
"Yes'm, right now."
"All right," she concluded. "I'll be right over."

Stopping only to remove her apron, pick up a nearby sweater, and give us instructions on "dishing up supper," she hurried out of the house.

Only two weeks later, Muzzie and the coach had to go through the very same routine, though this time it was the other shoulder. But the third time was different. No doubt the coach couldn't go through the ordeal again. He took Bob to the hospital, had the X-rays taken, waited until the doctor had set the bone and put the bandages and cast in place, and then drove Bob home.

We were just sitting down to supper when the doorbell rang. I was nearest the door and ran to open it. What I saw made me step back quickly and hold the door open *wide*.

There stood Bob, grinning weakly and with difficulty. His face was bruised and battered, one eye a real shiner and almost closed. He had deep scratches across one cheek and thick swollen lips. And, of course, one arm was in a sling.

Supporting him on one side was the coach, looking at Muzzie with an almost hangdog expression. On the other side was the young assistant coach, gazing in at us all as though *we* were the surprising sight, just because we all were half-standing and staring with dropped jaws toward the open door.

The coach nodded at Muzzie's look, which said better than words, *Tell me it isn't so, but of course, I know it is.* What she really said was much like a moan, "Oh no! Not again!"

Once again, we gathered around our conquering hero as he was carefully deposited on the couch and vied with each other to make him comfortable.

However, I couldn't appreciate this "heroic" stuff for long. "I didn't mind when you broke your left collar bone, but darn it! You had to go and break the right one, and now you can't cut the bread, and *I* have to do it!"

Bread-cutting was always Bob's job; gravy-making was mine. Judgment was served with each slice of bread as to its proper size as was the gravy judged for lumpiness or smoothness. Andy mashed the potatoes and beat them to velvety smoothness, and if anyone found even one lump, it was commented on throughout the meal.

These jobs demanded dexterity and talent, and we chosen ones (the jobs were handed down as time passed) gave our "all" to the operation.

In those days people didn't rush out to the car to take an injured person to the hospital. Few people had a car. We did, but Dad had it with him all week. As it was, Muzzie just dried her hands, took off her apron, and led the injured boy the four and a half blocks to the hospital. We were lucky—a hospital and only four and half blocks away.

Andy was the one with the brittle bones, and trouble seemed to dog his footsteps. He broke his leg from merely tumbling off a fence—the same fence that the rest of us fell off many times and got nothing worse from it than a few bumps or bruises. And later, in high school, he was frequently carried off the football field with a broken leg, arm or shoulder bone.

John was one of the best quarterbacks we had, and because he was short, he could wiggle through holes that weren't there.

Jim too was a football hero. He played hard but with such good nature that the effort wasn't noticeable.

Tom played football well but was frequently hurt and developed many complications from these bruises. He didn't complain about them.

Jake "Chakie" Dundore was our Pennsylvania Dutch Latin teacher. He worked with his big, hulking football players, forcing the Latin in them through their very pores so that they would pass and could play in the games. He was thin, slow-spoken, and gently and sometimes pointedly sarcastic, he smiled as he chided in class, "Gif the ball to Snyder. He'll take it through," or "Now, Mr. Reedt, do you plan to ride your pony"—the Latin translation—"or read from it?" He must always have been an old-young man because his hair was always white. He never rode but walked everywhere and was a great football fan and the best rooter that Sunbury High had.

Bob and Andy worked on the ice truck during the summer to get into trim for football. We always waited for it, and the kids in the neighborhood gathered round for bits and pieces of shaved ice.

One enterprising man in the neighborhood started a hokeypokey two-cents apiece ice-cream business, and it flourished. His tinkling bell called us each evening from the front porch swing, and we scrambled madly for our pennies.

SLAM THE DOOR SOFTLY

From the front porch, we listened to the Katydids and smelled the bread baking at the Butter Krust Bakery. When that happened, the whole gang gathered some pennies and bought the "rejects" (bread, sticky buns, etc.)—hot, soft, and delectable—and feasted.

At the Pretzel Factory, a tiny one room with huge ovens set into the brick wall, we bought for a few cents a huge bag of broken pretzels.

Eleven children and two parents made us a *lucky thirteen*. We reveled in that, mainly because the number seemed to shock most people, and if given a choice, each of us invariably chose that one. The boys proudly wore the huge number 13 on the backs of their football uniforms, and we girls felt extra superior in pointing them out to our friends.

This lack of respect for one superstition naturally prepared us for flaunting *all* superstitions. Black cat crossing our path, so what? Never walk under a ladder, crazy nonsense. Spill the salt shaker, clean it up!

When Bob borrowed Bea's hand mirror and then dropped and broke it, he called downstairs, "Hey, Bea. I broke your mirror. Sorry."

There was a sudden silence below stairs, then Bea shouted back, "Oh, Bob, you dummy! That's the only one I had." There was another moment of silence, and, "Well, okay. Clean it up, and you owe me a new one—*this week.*"

Superstitious? Never. We were thirteen!

We had to take our schooling seriously, and anyone coming home with really bad marks was almost drummed out of the family. We were sympathetic to one whom we felt had had a raw deal, but for failure to study or to "use our brains," there was none. "Hah, try to get sympathy here!" the mistreated one would growl self-pityingly. And always the answer would be, "I know where you'll find it—in the dictionary."

But when I came home with my final report card at the end of fifth grade and weepingly showed Muzzie the bright-red 40 in the arithmetic exam, the whole family was worriedly silent. "I'll flunk on that, Muzzie, and I know I didn't do that badly in the exam." I was so hurt and bewildered that I turned my face to the wall where I stood.

Muzzie, achingly sympathetic, tried to find some comfort for me, and suggested, tentatively "Well, maybe your teacher made a mistake, dear. Why don't you go to her tomorrow and ask what happened?"

"Oh, I couldn't!" I said. "She'd be furious because I doubted her."

But Muzzie prevailed, and the next day, I approached my teacher.

Miss K. looked up my marks and turned beet red. "Oh my goodness, I'm sorry! I copied the wrong mark onto your report card. You got a 70."

Our little ones played happily all summer long, but those approaching school age anxiously questioned the older ones about it. Invariably, someone would tell the approaching first grader, "You won't like Miss _____. She's mean to her pupils."

One small fish was very worried and confided his fears to Muzzie.

She assured him that school was a good and happy place to go and advised him, "Start out intending to like her, and then you probably will. Just tune in to her voice only, and all will be well."

He went quaveringly to his first day at school and followed Muzzie's advice. Much to his relief, he *did* like the teacher and school, and all was well.

Getting to school on time was a real chore for me.

"Hey, Mart, you'd better hurry, or you'll be late for school." Andy reminded, grinning broadly at my predicament as he leaped past me down the stairs.

Grrrrrr. Didn't I know that? And wasn't I struggling desperately to tighten the long underwear around a resisting leg with one hand and hold it until I would work the long cotton stocking up over it. I finally got the two little ones finished and was working on Tommy's last leg.

"It's a pretty big bump back there," seven-year-old Tommy observed mildly, holding up his right leg for closer inspection. And truly it was a bump, but there was no time to do it over, and I almost howled in despair.

"I *know* it is! But you'll just have to pretend you grew some new muscles today. I *have* to leave for school now."

"A muscle? Down there?" he asked in his slow husky voice but, seeing my near-explosive state, hastily added, "Okay. It's a muscle."

We'd been sitting on the stairs to perform this long-stocking-over-long-underwear operation because it was warmer there than in the bedrooms. And, of course, traffic down and up again for forgotten things and down again had been heavier than usual. Each time Bob, Andy, John, and Jim zipped past us, we'd had to, "Move over, you're blocking the aisle," and that was the real reason I was late. By the third request to move, I was seething.

"You fellas make me sick!" I grated, sliding in close to the wall and at the same time keeping a firm grip on stocking and underwear. "You gang up on the bathroom so we girls can't use it," I snapped. "Then you eat a good, hearty breakfast," I went on with heavy sarcasm, "and go off to school—free as the birds."

And as each pair of long legs slid past me, I received the usual baiting reply. "Yup," they drawled contentedly, "tha's right," and each in turn gave me a quick pat on my head as a parting shot.

My fury knew no bounds, but I couldn't catch them as I still wasn't completely dressed. And I couldn't take it out on Tommy, the last of my little "problems."

I planted a quick kiss on the top of his head and sent him downstairs. "Go right to the kitchen and eat your breakfast," I reminded as I raced up the stairs. "No stopping to read your new book! Now mind!"

I'd only time to put on my green plaid dress—it had the least number of buttons—run a comb through my hair again after the ruffling pats the boys had given me, grab my coat and books, and really *run* to school.

"Marney?" Muzzie's voice followed me as I dashed for the door. "Your breakfast?"

"No time," I shouted and started my five-hundred-yard dash. Dad had called me "Legs" as I was growing up. "Like a colt," he'd often said, and I was glad for them now.

I made it.

Dad and his brother Sydney argued furiously on any and every subject, but their favorite topic was politics. Fast, furious, loud, and angry, their energetic anger was always ready for a new round the next time the Snydey Snyder's came. That was "wild time" when Uncle Sydney and Aunt Pearl and their nine came to visit.

SLAM THE DOOR SOFTLY

Aunt Mable and Uncle John drove all the way from Washington, DC, to see us one Fourth of July! There were squeals and yells from us as we erupted from the house, and Muzzie had a huge smile on her face because she was so happy to see her sister. They were so pleasant and full of fun. Everyone rallied around to unload the backseat and trunk of their car, and they always brought a watermelon! There was so much fun and laughter! Muzzie had baked pies and pies and cakes and cakes and huge meat loaves and hams—oh, how we ate. We all took turns turning the ice-cream freezer, and it was delicious, especially the paddle.

The whole neighborhood was included, and we became one huge family for that night—the oohs and aahs and sighs of delight at each new rocket, the lovely unexpected colors, the sudden bomb-like crash that made us jump in delighted fear, the daring boys who set the "crackers" alight and then ran, And the quiet contentment when all was over.

Some expressions that we kids used were, "Moley hoses!" "Holy cats!" "Banana oil!" "Baloney!" "It's the cat's whiskers!" "You're the cat's meow!" and "You got it bass-ackward!" Dad said, "Balderdash!" But his cuss word was "Consarn it!"

Muzzie taught us all her favorite poem, recited alternately by her and one of us:

> Good morning, glory.
> How do you dew, drop?
> Do you think it'll rain, dear?
> It may, flower."

Mary was the first to leave home to attend a nurses training school. Since it was nearby, she came home every other weekend full of advice and cautions about the dos and don'ts of the care of the sick. We soon learned to take her instructions with several grains of salt, for invariably, her next visit would void the instructions of a previous visit. For instance, on her first visit, she would proclaim, "Use the hot-water bottle on a sore spot to ease the pain." Her next visit would add, "Except in case of pain in the lower right side, then use an ice pack—it may be appendicitis." If after the first visit one of us had been felled by appendicitis, it behooved us to wait until her second visit to really learn how to treat it. Thank goodness, we had our family doctor to call upon.

Then Bea went away to college, and the first few weeks, we were deluged with her letters. Muzzie would sit in her rocker and read the letters aloud to all of us gathered around, and a slow tear would slip down her cheek.

"Poor Bea" she would say, "she's homesick."

Then the rest of us would sniff and blow our noses, and thinking of "poor Bea" so far away from home, we instinctively drew closer to one another and to Muzzie.

She couldn't come home every weekend as Mary could because her school was too far away. But Dad fixed that. When he came home and found us all so mournful, he said, "Well, come on, pile into the car. We'll go to see her." And we did. Our car, like the house, learned to "give" a little to make room for yet one more.

After that, Bea was all right. Now her letters almost always contained a request for a batch of Muzzie's cookies. "I've bet so many cookies, and I've lost so many bets," she wrote, "that I really need a *big* batch, Muzzie."

SLAM THE DOOR SOFTLY

Each in their turn, Bob and Andy left for college. As well as working toward their degrees, they, what else, played football!

I had gone up to Penn State for a house-party weekend and went to the football game with a boyfriend to see my brothers play, Bob on the first string and Andy on the second string.

To my horror, Bob was knocked out and carried off the field. I was worried and apprehensive but waited in the stands. Suddenly taps were sounded at half-time, and a woman near me said, "Oh…h…h. Did that poor boy die?"

That did it! I almost fainted! I bolted from the stands, followed by my boyfriend, and raced around the back to reach the dressing rooms. There I found Andy, alone, crying.

We held each other tightly, hoping for the best but fearing the worst. Finally, the coach appeared, looking gaunt and worn. Seeing our stricken faces, he immediately came over and said, "Bob will be all right, although he's badly injured."

The relief was so great that I felt dizzy.

"We're taking him to the hospital now, and you can come too if you wish," the coach added.

We crowded into the ambulance with Bob and, during that long ride, never spoke a single word while keeping our eyes glued to his face. After he woke, in the hospital with all of his bones set, Andy and I looked at each other and said in unison, "What'll we tell Muzzie?"

Bob recovered enough to play many more games for his alma mater.

Dad was away all week working for the federal government, so when he came home on weekends, we walked the chalk line so that he wouldn't have to spoil the weekend for himself, Muzzie, and all of us with meting out punishments. He, in turn, was ever ready with requested or unrequested funds, maybe to make up for not seeing us all week.

His first car was an Overland, and a real beauty. He began taking driving lessons, and just as we were getting out of school one day, who should we see but Dad bucking along the street just like a cowboy on a bucking bronco. Feeling indignant that he should appear so undignified before all the kids (who made no bones about shouting, "Put a nickel in it," "Get a horse!" and "Ride 'em, cowboy!"), we hurriedly ducked up the alley so no one could see us.

Squeezing thirteen people into our little house was a problem, but not nearly the problem we had with squeezing that many into a five-passenger car. Naturally, someone had to hold someone. In fact, everyone had to hold someone, sometimes as many as three deep, making the bottom fellows' view of the countryside around pigtails quite limited.

It was not to the liking of the older ones to be seen like a band of gypsies going for a Sunday-afternoon drive, so one by one, the numbers fell off. At last, the seating arrangements became quite comfortable, as well as the view.

When you are one of eleven children you learn to take turns, not to "tattle" on one another, and to hope for a drumstick on "chicken day." Still, you know darn well that you'll probably end up with a wing because you are no longer one of the "little ones." You'd think, because they *were* little, that their stomachs wouldn't need as much meat as our bigger ones, but the rule had always been "the little ones get the drumsticks and you've had *your* turn." But we couldn't help eyeing the little monsters with real envy as they bit eagerly and happily into the luscious delicacy.

On those rare occasions (usually only on Thanksgiving and Christmas) when we had turkey, we *stuffed* ourselves as full as the turkey itself, and *who needed* the drumsticks?

To leave the table at any time for a missing condiment or a refill was risky business. The boys were ever ready to steal from the missing person's plate and then, with complete innocence, go on eating. The knew *nothing* about the missing food, and the "missing person" could screech her head off—no one tattled.

I was one of those not-too-bright-ones, a "dreamer" as I was called so often, who had a set pattern for eating. First, I ate all the required and not-especially-liked foods and saved the best 'til last. That was my undoing, but I never seemed to learn. I would trim all the fat from a slice of roast beef or ham and eat all the less succulent parts first, with the delicate morsel I most wanted lying, waiting, in the exact center of my plate. Then with my fork directed toward it in delightful anticipation, I was invariably hoodwinked out of it by one of my inventive brothers, who suddenly shouted that we must, "Look! Look!" at something strange going on outside, under the table, or on the ceiling. I couldn't help it. I *had* to look. And when it was agreed by all that the excitement wasn't all that wonderful, I'd return to my last bite, and of course, it was gone.

Bea developed her own method for dealing with this problem, shocking everyone the first time she did it, but secretly delighting in her ingenuity.

This particular meal, we were having pork chops, and as was her usual custom, Bee ate around the meaty loin section, saving it for last. She started to get up to go to the sink and wash her hands, which were slightly greasy from handling the bone. But she stopped in midair, glanced around at us and then, a crafty gleam in her eye, stood up for all to see, picked up the precious loin morsel that she had saved and, with delicate sweeping strokes, ran her tongue over the meat. Triumphantly, she then laid it back in the center of her plate.

Muzzie was, for the moment, shocked speechless, then, "Ooooooh! Bea...a...trice!"

Bob's eyes grinned even as he uttered his "Ugh! How dirty can you get?"

But the sounds of disapproval from the whole assemblage, the little ones echoing the sounds because they believed it was expected of them, didn't shame Bea. She was grinning with joy at having bested the boys.

"It'll be here when I come back," she said smugly, and there was no denying that fact.

After that, Bea's plate was left strictly alone. No one could actually be sure that she hadn't already put her "stamp" on the contents of her plate.

When we had company for a meal, we had special signals. If there was plenty of that particular food, it was MIK ("More in kitchen"); if it was going down too fast, it was FHB ("Family hold back").

We never had elbow room at our table, no matter how many leaves were added to extend it, but somehow there always was room for one more or two or even three more. One motherless boy was an especial favorite of Muzzie's, and although he had a family and meals to go home to, he enjoyed eating with us, and Muzzie was determined to fatten him up. So Bill became one of us, and his torn shirts or pants were often a part of the big pile of mending that Muzzie tackled daily.

To be a guest at our table was hazardous, unless they were friends or business acquaintances of Dad. Others had to watch out for the "buttered thumb" or "missing tidbit from the plate." Watermelon was finally relegated to the lawn outside because of too many seed battles. We always took the measure of the victim first to see how far we could go and how much of a sense of humor they had before initiating them. Those reared in more genteel surroundings were invariably scared off by the boys, who had no sympathy for any girl who couldn't pet a white mouse or touch a garter snake.

Our new physical education teacher, Gwen Spangenberg, had gone to Bea's school, and this was her first teaching job. Muzzie invited her to the house, and we "absorbed" her into the family. At her first dinner with us, when the usual passing of the dishes was over, she hesitantly asked for the butter. Little did she know that it had purposely been held back so that she would have to ask for it. Now the butter began its trip around the table, and all eyes concentrated on their plates. The dish reached her in good time, and she reached out to accept it—overreached, she thought, much to her embarrassment. Her thumb was deeply imbedded in the butter. Her hasty glance around the table reassured her that she hadn't been observed. Then one by one, grinning faces turned toward her. The laughter was long and loud, and she was initiated into the family. She was a good sport and readily joined in.

She took her role as "big sister" very seriously. Not only did she pitch in with the washing of dishes, diapering a baby or wielding a dry mop, she also felt that she should do her part in teaching us the "facts of life." She loved us all and wanted only the best in life for each of us.

At the time, each of us thought that *he* was the chosen one and always listened respectfully. After all, she was one of our teachers as well as a foster big sister, but at the same time, we nearly died laughing inwardly, knowing that we could probably tell her a thing or two about the "facts."

Many years later, when we compared notes we found that she'd cornered each of us and delivered her message. But Jonnie's was the most original locale—straining at the oars in a rowboat as he took her across the river to Sandy Beach where everyone was swimming. "Heck," he said. "How could I get away from her out in the middle of the river?" Jonnie was always the elusive one when it was time for a lecture, and she must have waited a long time to catch him.

Bea's first date drove a sports car. She begged Muzzie very seriously to keep us out of sight until they left. "It's so embarrassing," she'd moan. "They flock around like a bunch of chickens, and I feel like shooing them away."

One of Bea's dates, a quiet fellow unused to so many in one family, had a lovely habit of bringing her flowers or candy. The flowers were okay, but they never had much "holding power" for us kids. We'd see them and then go quietly about our business. But a bag of candy! Well, that was something else again! No one had to pass the word; we just *knew* when he brought candy and not by smelling, either. Like healthy ghosts, we suddenly would appear as Bea opened the candy bag, and of course, for his benefit, to show him what a polite girl she was, she offered us some candy. Seething, slowly boiling inside, she stood smilingly holding the bag as one by one we divested it of its succulent contents. But then we always left a few pieces for Bea and her friend. It wasn't polite to eat the last few pieces. He was quiet and a slow thinker, but he finally caught on after the third or fourth bag. Then he kept it in his car and gave it to her after they'd pulled away from the house.

Quarantine signs were frequently on our front door. They were used on our house so often that the health officer, who was also the truant officer, finally left the tacks on the front of the house. "Might as well just hook the sign on the same tacks. Better than wastin' 'em."

Muzzie nursed three and four at a time. Measles and chicken pox were frequent visitors, and she'd go from bed to bed trying to ease the terrible whoops that shook us. When one of us came down with a disease, the rest followed suit so that we usually were quarantined for at least two months instead of two weeks.

Muzzie took it all with patience and kept us in good humor. If it ever became too overwhelming, we seldom knew it. If she wept, it was alone.

But one quarantine left us all sick at the beginning and completely bored at the end—scarlet fever. Jonnie was so sick that Muzzie moved into his room to care for him, and Mary, now a nurse, took over the house and our care. She gave each of us a shot in our derrieres. We were so sick! One by one, we went to the bathroom to throw up. Afterward, Jonnie slowly sank into the empty bathtub, feet sticking out over the edge. Jimmie, on his way out after doing the same, eyed him, nodded, and made it to the next room where he fell onto my bed. Andy followed closely behind, and then Tommy.

I headed for my bed, saw that it was pretty crowded, and settled for the floor. Nausea was followed by great swelling hives! We were a mess!

Dad stayed at the hotel, but several times during the week, he came home and took the recovered ones out to the woods to run and yell.

All of our names were chosen from the Bible or from some well-read and much-loved story or poem that Dad was reading aloud to Muzzie. This almost nightly ritual was after we were all finished with our Bible reading and individual bedtime prayers and safely abed. In the peaceful hour or two left to them, Dad read aloud while Muzzie darned and mended, sharing the same table lamp, she softly rocking and he bending over the book, his voice rising and falling with inflection. Both sounds reached us in our upstairs bedrooms with a lulling feel of security.

They were both great readers, but babies took so much of Muzzie's time that she could seldom settle down to a book. This was Dad's solution to the problem, and they enjoyed their evenings together so much that through the years they had read a small library.

Through this love of books and some of their many characters, we received some pretty fancy names. It wasn't hard to figure out what they'd been reading before the new baby was born. For the most part, we were given biblical names for the Bible was the most read and most important book in our house. But the classics, good novels, history, and poetry all had a place in our lives.

Sometimes we were named for a good friend or acquaintance, and in one case, as we teased Muzzie and Dad, it backfired.

Their motives were pure when they gave Andy the middle name of *Beitzel* after a good friend, a confirmed bachelor. But we always kidded them that to pin an outlandish name like that on an innocent baby, they had to have an ulterior motive such as "expecting him to inherit."

The hilarious laughter that filled the house the day Dad came home and announced, "Mr. Beitzel has taken him a wife," has never been matched.

It was fun. Being one of eleven children was an experience, an up-and-down experience to be sure, but it was also a glorious one. We fought like young tigers *with* one another and *for* one another if an outsider was so foolish as to take on one of us in a fight! The enemy always went away bruised and battered. He should have known better in the first place than to tackle one of us.

Then there were the moments of peace and joy, the singing together and playing together, and the laughter. They were the joyous moments, and they were the salve to our battle scars when we disagreed, for our laughter was as real and spontaneous as our anger. Muzzie always mournfully declared, "They are all made of quicksilver. Not one is able to take the middle ground. They're either at the heights," she contended, "or down in the deepest depths."

She was as nearly saintly as any human being I ever knew, but God never meant for a real saint to live on earth, and for that I am grateful. Muzzie was not a saint, but it took a lot of bickering and quarreling and fooling around on our part before she really flew off the handle. When she did, we felt as though a hurricane had struck! Orders flew thick and fast, and woe unto the slow mover! On those days, the house got scrubbed and polished and waxed until it shone, and we ached! But we should have learned because her belief never changed that "idle hands—and children—get into trouble."

It wasn't as though we ever had any peace and quiet. With eleven children in one small house, all rushing, yelling and shouting, quarreling (or laughing—each with a heartier laugh than the last), peace just naturally gave us a wide berth.

Muzzie learned through the years that song *did* solve that problem most of the time. Her songs turned usually to church and Sunday-school hymns, and she could find a fitting one for each occasion.

When we procrastinated on a job, she'd start up, "Work, for the night is coming. Work, for the day is done…" A gentle reminder would be "Idle Hands." If we snapped or snarled at one another, it was "Love One Another." "Onward Christian Soldiers" always set us to working faster when we were too slow and time was catching up with us.

Muzzie adopted people and never seemed to remember any act of kindness she had performed in the past, no matter if that past was only yesterday. She had a grand sense of humor, was quick with a quip, and never needed to have a good joke explained. She laughed often, such a delicious laugh that we all joined in.

She was our lodestar—the shining light to whom we all turned in good times and bad. We loved her without reserve, and she returned that love a thousandfold and enveloped us all in warmth and brightness.

Cast of Characters

Dad (Vernon Gywnne Snyder)–Earned and received our great respect, though we were as reticent as he to *show* our love and affection.

Mother (Carrie Estella "Muzzie" Snyder)–A saint on earth with a marvelous singing voice, a laugh that was beautifully catching, and a sense of justice backed up by her complete and simple faith in God.

Mary Estella ("Mamie")–Muzzie agreed to passing down her middle name because "it wasn't too bad." A lady, a romantic, and a dreamer. Too often up in the clouds, and dinner could and *did* burn because of it when she was chief cook. As the no. 1 child, she was the guinea pig for the rest of us. She fought the good fight for silk stockings, lipstick, and boyfriends, and we younger girls got all the benefits.

Ruth Elizabeth ("Ruthie")–Our never-to-grow baby who died at two weeks of age. We never knew her, but we loved her our Baby Ruthie.

Beatrice Eleanor ("Bea," "Bee," "Beacie," "Beat")–The tomboy. She regularly beat up the boys in the neighborhood, could walk the back fence without falling, and played football and baseball. Anything the boys could do she could do better. Femininity was a bad word where she was concerned.

Robert Gwynne ("Bob"): Dad allowed the use of his middle name. "Head man," protector, advisor, judge, referee, and doctor were all roles he played in Dad's absence and, when necessary, chief "lowerer of the boom." He mended our toys, our broken hearts and gave us sound advice.

Andrew Bietzel ("Andy")–*Beitzel* from a rich Mr. Bietzel, who turned traitor by marrying and having his own children. Studied hard and made his grades and honors on his own. Followed Bob but became his own man in spite of that and a football star in his own right.

Martha Evangeline ("Marney," "Mart," "Butch," "Teacher")–*Evangeline* from the poem of the same name. Mother's helper. Constantly correcting the younger children's grammar. Hated dirty stories. Undecided whether to be a movie actress, opera singer, or interior decorator. Always dramatic, and her most used line was "Someday I'm going to go somewhere without having to drag along five or six kids."

John Howard ("Jonnie")–Middle name from a good friend named Howard. Artistic—could make anything from "nothing" and it was perfect. The shortest of the boys and angry about it. A fighter in the belief that *that* made up for his lack of height. "Oh, for cryin' out loud!"

James Edwin ("Jimmie," "Jim")–The happy boy. Easygoing, quick laughter, generous and kind. A good companion who was equally happy playing alone or with a crowd. Self-sufficient even as a child.

Thomas Leon ("Tommy," "Tom")–Good little businessman. Had money when all others were broke. Charged interest on a loan. We grumbled but paid up—Dad enjoyed this. Good and dear, very serious.

Vernon Gwynne Jr. ("Noonie")–Finally a junior! Muzzy finally prevailed upon Dad to give a son his name. A happy boy. Tall, gangly, skinny. "Nooner" was as close as he could pronounce "junior," so he finally became "Noon," or twelve o'clock. Always a fast talker because he was in a great hurry to share his latest knowledge but garbled his words and one of us had to say "Hold it. Now begin again."

Winifred Esther ("Winnie")–*Winifred* for a very good friend of the family. The baby girl. Looked like a little Indian papoose when born. Sensitive and sweet. Too easily hurt. Needed much loving—and usually got it.

George Frederick–I was allowed the honor of choosing his middle name. Gruff sometimes but quite able to get along alone. Pleasant when left to his own devices. Had a demon in his eyes or the Old Nick. A devil-may-care attitude, "So it didn't work.

Memories

Recollections of Beatrice Eleanor Snyder Zimmerman (April 1995)

Most people used the word *"charming"* to describe my father, Vernon Gwynne Snyder. He impressed my college friends tremendously with his charm and impeccable dress. He always taught and insisted on honesty in his children. If any one of us was found to be untruthful, it was down to the basement with us where he chastised us thoroughly with a plaster lathe on our backside. He was a perfectionist, and an amateur cabinetmaker. He loved to make things with his hands.

One Christmas when I was about six years old, he made a child's dining room set for the four children which he then had. It consisted of a table, four chairs, and a sideboard. The sideboard had a mirror on the top and two shelves on the bottom behind two doors. Across the top he had put a shelf, which was held in place by brackets. We loved that furniture. To make our happiness complete, our grandmother Margaret E. Frownfelter, gave us a set of glass dishes to put in the sideboard. They were clear, with a cutout diamond design, and resemble a pattern that today is called "American." I still have the butter, creamer, and sugar dishes from that set.

My father had aspired to be a minister when he was young, and left us under the impression that his mother had discouraged it because of lack of funds. He read the Bible to the family every morning. At the morning devotions, we children knelt to pray at our own chair. We lived beside the parsonage of the church which we attended in Penbrook, and were very active in church services and activities. He was very fussy that the words which we used were well-chosen and that our speech was grammar-perfect. An appropriate book, chosen by him, was to be expected each Christmas, birthday, and holiday; and they were excellent.

When I was small, he helped to sing in the church choir. Although he and my mother only completed the eighth grade, he claimed to be a "self-made man." He was an avid student and read incessantly. He was excellent with words and had discriminating taste.

Recollections from Malcolm Putnam Brown (April 15, 1981)

My father-in-law, V. G. Snyder—always aristocratic in bearing, a banker by profession—told me of an incident when he was first married.

A local water company was just forming in Penbrook (the suburb of Harrisburg where they lived), and they wanted to replace his well with a municipal water supply. The representative from the water company assured him that the maximum cost would be $2.00/month, so he had it installed. The meter was in the front yard, underground and with a wooden cover. The man had told VG how the meter was read, so after half a month had passed, VG read the meter and saw that the cost was already over $3.00. He closed the cutoff valve, took a pipe wrench, removed the meter, and reversed it until a day or so before the meter was due to be read. He then put it back to its original position. The monthly bill was $2.00. Thereafter, all the years he lived there, he reversed it for ten days a month, and the bill was always what he had been promised.

He was a very complicated man. He was a devotee of Father Coughlin, a Roman Catholic priest who advocated designed inflation to allow the poor to pay off their debts with printed money and start afresh.

Excerpts from a story written by Mary Estella Snyder Burrows Poeth for her church magazine:

> While talking with her one day she was reminiscing about her girlhood. Her family had pretty rough sledding and, being the eldest of nine children, she had to go to work at an early age. She was deprived of a high school education, but she never complained about this. When she was sixteen or seventeen years old she started singing in a church choir and, with her beautiful voice, soon became soloist there. With the help of the organist she learned to read music to a fair degree. Choir work seemed to be her only social outlet, but in a few years she met a man of her choice. The Board of Governors of the church wanted to send her to a special music school and pay all her expenses because they felt that she had the potential to be a great singer, but she refused them in order to marry and raise a family.

As was the custom in those days, she bore her children at home with the help of a practical nurse to care for her and the baby, and to cook and clean. She praised these women highly, except for one who brought her own little boy with her. This little fellow ran in and out of the kitchen door, sometimes leaving it open, when his mother was bathing the new baby (Ruth) in front of the kitchen fire. Consequently the baby became ill with pneumonia and died. Even then she never censured the woman for allowing this, but always regretted not being able to raise that child.

Many times she and I would entertain the neighbors with our duets while working around the house. First one neighbor would call and say "Will you two please sing this or that?", and then another would call across the yard asking for another hymn or tune.

One day while we were singing a tramp came to the door and asked for some food. She prepared a plate of whatever she was cooking and handed it to him. The tramp had eaten, and she thought that he had gone, when he called to her and asked if we could sing "What a Friend We Have in Jesus", adding that his mother used to sing it. Of course she obliged and, while we were singing, took a broom and quietly swept all the walks around the house.

She never missed tucking the youngest children in bed and listening to their tales of the day. I never heard her tell my father of their misdeeds when he arrived home.

When I was twelve years old I wanted a new dress for Christmas. Times were tough just then, so she took her wedding dress out of mothballs and made me a jumper. Many nights she stayed up until

1 or 2 a.m. to finish a dress for one of her daughters, or a shirt or pants for one of her sons, even though she was dead tired.

Her unselfishness was beyond compare. If she heard of a needy person she would scrounge around for bits of material for clothing for them, or cook a meal, or take care of another's sick child or relative.

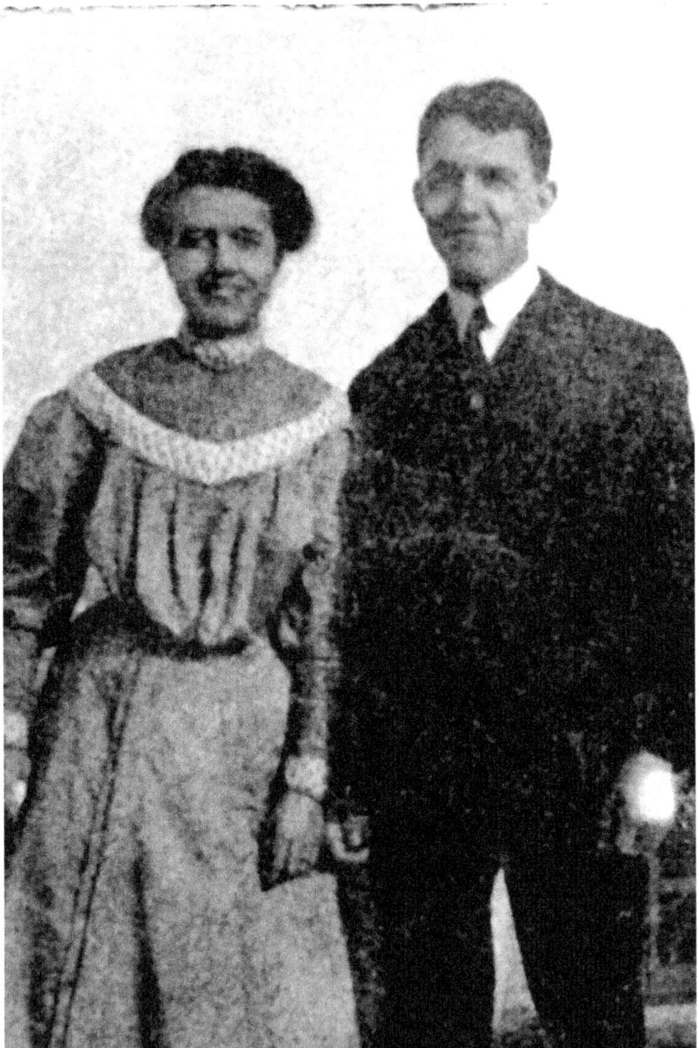

SLAM THE DOOR SOFTLY

MARTHA SNYDER BROWN

SLAM THE DOOR SOFTLY

MARTHA SNYDER BROWN

SLAM THE DOOR SOFTLY

MARTHA SNYDER BROWN

SLAM THE DOOR SOFTLY

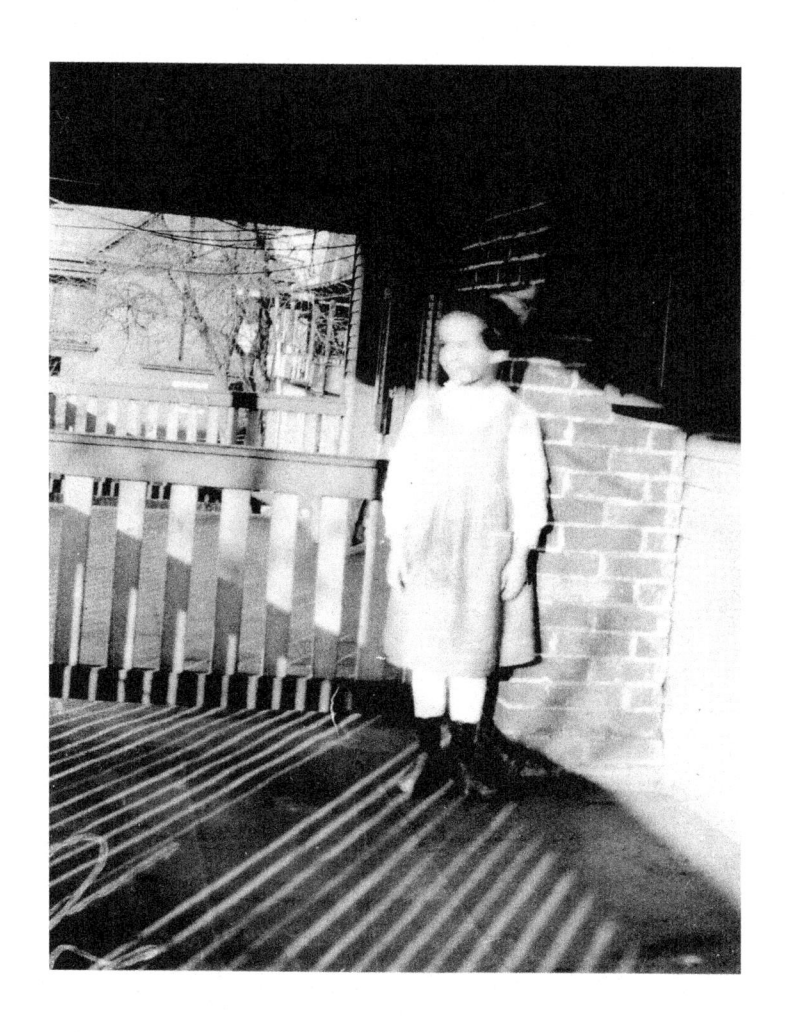

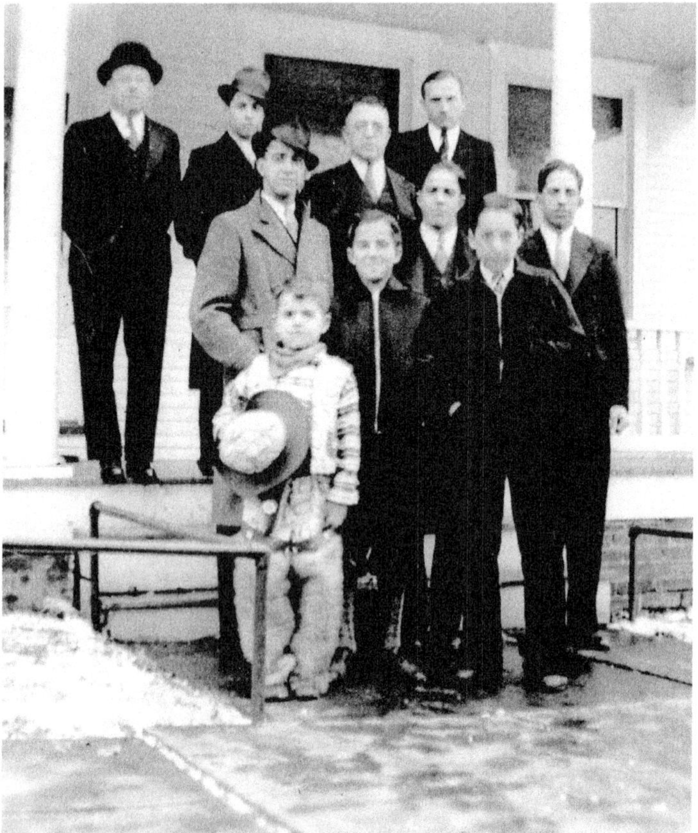

SLAM THE DOOR SOFTLY

MARTHA SNYDER BROWN

SLAM THE DOOR SOFTLY

MARTHA SNYDER BROWN

SLAM THE DOOR SOFTLY

MARTHA SNYDER BROWN

SLAM THE DOOR SOFTLY

MARTHA SNYDER BROWN

SLAM THE DOOR SOFTLY

MARTHA SNYDER BROWN

SLAM THE DOOR SOFTLY

MARTHA SNYDER BROWN

SLAM THE DOOR SOFTLY

MARTHA SNYDER BROWN

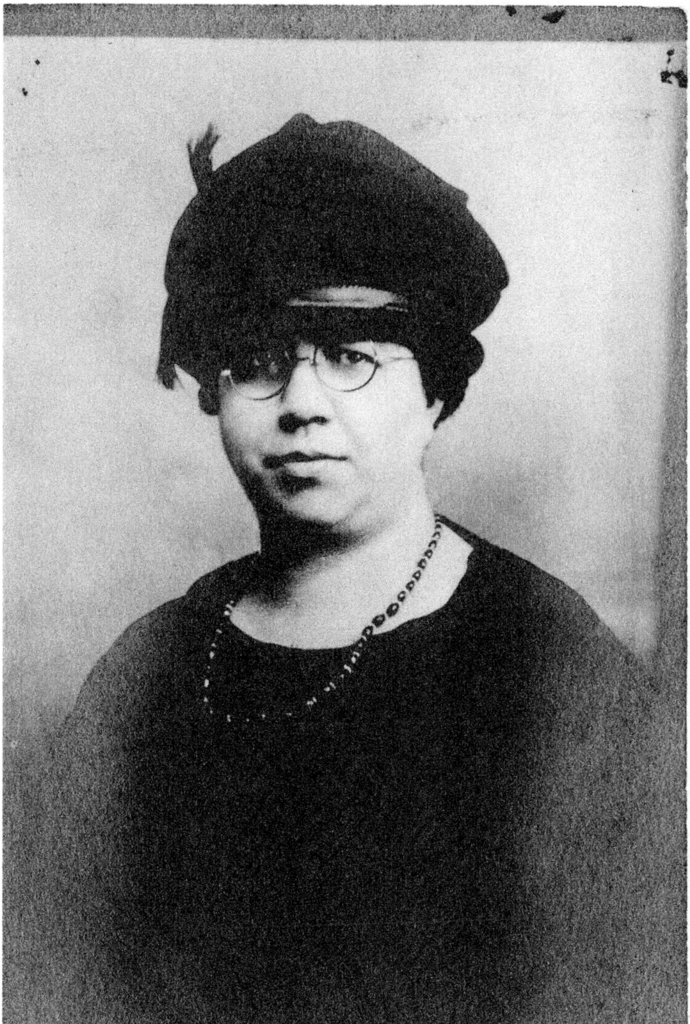

MARTHA SNYDER BROWN

SLAM THE DOOR SOFTLY

CPSIA information can be obtained at www.ICGtesting.com
Printed in the USA
LVOW04s1514030415

433204LV00014B/355/P

9 781634 491242